W9-DIW-580

Daniel Erasmus

# The future of ICT in financial services

## The Rabobank ICT scenarios

A DTN scenario thinking casebook DTN 2008

Publisher: DTN Press
Prinsengracht 707
1017 JW, Amsterdam, Netherlands
Tel. +31 428 4190
www.dtn.net
info@dtn.net

Design: Nana Manojlovic, Bouwe van der Molen
DTP: Nana Manojlovic, Mustafa Özbek
Visualisation: Annika Varjonen, Visual Impact

Printed in the Netherlands by
Drukkerij Koenders & Van Steijn, Badhoevedorp

ISBN: 978-90-79682-01-0

Daniel Erasmus

# The future of ICT in financial services

## The Rabobank ICT scenarios

# Table of contents

# Foreword

Three years ago Rabo Group ICT came into being. It was a fresh start for everyone, and for us as Management Team (MT) for "Systeemrealisatie" (the systems development department), it meant beginning with a whole new team. Together we sought a subject that would move us to think beyond the scope of our daily concerns—a topic we could work on periodically, away from our routine tasks; a subject through which we could work on the future of a new department; a strategic subject that was appropriate to our place and function within the organisation and to the future of what we do. We wanted to get an overview of our future as the ICT development department.

In order to do this properly, it is of vital importance to thoroughly know the role and function of ICT in financial institutions. Getting this into the right perspective can help us set goals as a department, justify investments in people and departments, and build a robust strategy for Systeemrealisatie.

We chose scenario analyses as a method because it allows us to recognise uncertainties, look at the future in different ways and review investments in the light of different views on the future. With that you create a robust strategy that still allows for flexibility—important attributes in a constantly changing world. We have reviewed our investment choices in developing a coherent system, methods, outsourcing and knowledge building in the context of the scenarios we developed in the process, thus linking daily practice to visions of the future.

Over the course of two years, we worked on the scenarios one day every two months, under the professional guidance of Daniel Erasmus and his team at the DTN. These were inspiring workshops that generated a lot of pleasure, new ideas and memorable evenings. We worked hard in good cooperation with one another in the workshops, and that gave us energy and many new insights. Altogether, we worked for 10 full days—which is not a lot, in fact, when we take the results into account. But a lot of the preparations, reporting and final work was done by Daniel and his team.

Sharing the results is probably the hardest task. As MT Systeemrealisatie we have experienced this process together; we watched and commented on the interviews; we discussed and drew conclusions. This is an experience that we would like to share with others, but that isn't easy. We organised some workshops on different elements of the scenario process. It gives other people some idea, but it doesn't provide the full insights that we would like to share with them. I hope this book will contribute to a more complete sharing of our experience, at least as far as the content is concerned. I hope the game will help to get a feel of the scenario method.

In the years ahead we will come together about twice a year to review current developments in light of the scenarios to sharpen our strategic choices and visions. It is a great and inspiring process!

Rob Klomps

# Acknowledgments


A number of things came together to make this case history possible. Without doubt, the first was Rabobank's decision to take an expedition into scenario thinking about the future of ICT and financial services. It is a credit to the progressive outlook of Rabobank Nederlands that it took the opportunity to go outside the frame of business-as-usual to stretch its imagination and to develop new ways to think about changing circumstances. The second decisive factor was the success of the endeavor. It was a rigorous and challenging process, and there were no simple guarantees for success. Next was the Rabobank team—great partners for DTN to work with: the team members worked hard, kept open minds, continually challenged themselves and made it a fun and successful journey. And last, the bank's interest in sharing the learning and experience with others made this book possible.

My special thanks, then, to Rabobank Nederlands and to the members of the Rabobank Systeemrealisatie team:

(core workshop participants)

**Rob Klomps**—for keeping an eye on the horizon and his feet on the ground, and for his trusted friendship

**Pieter Ketting**—for emphasizing the transformation of the larger group of SR managers and our memorable journey to the North

**Jos Mijnen**—for bringing his sharp new insights, humour and love of good wine into the process

**Jeanne Driessen**—for her clear, consistent thinking and sharing her Millennial son's remarkable creativity at a key moment in the process

**Margreet Oostenbrink**—for her love of good food, and her emphasis on stretching our strategic thinking into new places

**Mark Hese**—for keeping the numbers sound

**Sjaak Oosterveer**—for keeping our thinking practical and effectual

**Rob Bakker**—for being the glue in the process, and for insisting that we order snacks for 20 people in a workshop with only 10 participants

**Wil Leeuwis**—for his openness to learning new ideas and his seriousness about understanding ICT deeply from Cobol to PHP

The following additional people from Rabobank did not participate in the workshops, but shared their insights in interviews:

**Rik Op den Brouw**—for always thinking two steps ahead

**Pieter Canton**—for keeping the history of ICT at Rabobank

**Pieter Fortuijn**—for clear insight into the growth of the jobs market in Europe

**Rob Kemna**—for his insights into ICT and outsourcing

**Mariëlle Lichtenberg**—for her insights into the human dimension of ICT

**Marjo Smulders**—for her insight into the framing of ICT and the key question about how a new generation will use these technologies

**Toine Straathof**—for a view on the bold CRM initiative at Rabobank

**Hans van Zanten**—for a view of large-scale ICT system maintenance

**Karin van den Brink**—for her patience in organising and, shall we say it gently, organic schedule over the last two years

We owe the success of the project to the "remarkable people" we interviewed. They freely gave their time and thoughts, bringing new perspectives and critical insights that challenged and enhanced our thinking about the focal issue. We thank:

**Ton van Asseldonk**—for sharing his intuition for complex systems
**Henk Badoux & Richard Dingemans**—for sharing the insights from SAP in the process
**David Bank**—for sharing a morning explaining his work to transform the perceived problem of aging baby boomers into an opportunity for social transformation
**Eddy Bex**—for his insight that outsourcing is becoming process oriented
**Michiel Boreel**—for a wonderful afternoon interview in the south of Amsterdam and insight into open innovation
**Natarajan Chandrasekaran**—for a fascinating morning in Bangalore, the rare gift of a 10-year view on matters, and a delicious lunch
**Peter Cochrane**—for his unique combination of being succinct, eloquent and insightful
**Vic d'Alfonso**—for sharing the learning of his journey to India
**Jack van Driel**—for asking some good hard questions
**Deepak Ghaisas**—for his insights into what makes Indian IT tick
**Christian Goeckenjan & Richard Lowrie**—for making time between presentations and excellent insight into how the industry could transform itself
**Ashwin Goyal**—for deep insight on a windy San Francisco afternoon
**Eric van Heck**—for mastering the art of being a professor with clear opinions
**Theo Huibers**—for bringing a clear view on next-generation interface technology into our thinking
**Brewster Kahle**—for his and Mary's hospitality in San Francisco, their friendship, and sharing his deep understanding of large-scale systems
**Heikki Karjaluoto**—for insights in Oolu, the place with the dubious claim of having invented SMS
**Jongwan Kim**—for our interview and boat ride on the river Han in Seoul, and for making me welcome in one of the most exciting countries in Asia
**Vivek Kulkarni**—for sharing his vision of Bangalore, and being one of the few people who have seen their vision become reality
**Praveen Kumar**—for sharing his insight into CRM and the view of a CIO
**Jaron Lanier**—for his crystal clear thinking, long interviews and a great lunch at O'Chama
**Peter Leyden**—for his friendship, help in setting up the interviews in California, and being an excellent host, who always makes you think of the world in a slightly different way
**Krish Murali Eswar**—for being one of the clearest and most logical thinkers of our journey
**Eric Rodenbeck**—for his tour through the Mission in San Francisco, and insight into new ways of seeing data
**Ralph Schonenbach & Severin Weiss**—for help in introducing me to some of the most interesting people in India who are heading this revolution, and for sharing the exciting work they are doing to support outsourcing at Tresle
**Rajeev Srivastava**—for welcoming me to India, and his keen eye for the big human picture
**Fred Studer**—for sharing his thoughts on developments at Oracle
**Anthony Townsend**—for his view as a Gen X investor and on the role that technology can play
**Eddy Vermeire**—for asking hard questions, and offering insightful answers

Despite the fact that it was an intellectual journey, it involved real travel and logistics—things known to harbour troublesome surprises. So, a special thanks to the people who showed me Mumbai and Bangalore and made me feel at home in heart and in mind; and to the staff of the **Triton Hotel** in San Francisco, the **Four Seasons** in Zurich and the **Taj Mahal Hotel** in Mumbai

Over the last 12 years now I have been building scenarios, a journey that would not have been possible without the encouragement of some of the superb people in this field—many of them formerly with Shell. Specifically I would like to thank **Arie de Geus**, for convincing me to start facilitating scenario processes in the first place; **Napier Collyns**, for keeping the stories alive; **Jay Ogilvy**, for creating thinking systems both of whom are currently with the GBillion; **Paul de Ruijter**,for his critical support, wonderful friendship and some of the original thinking relating to Fuzzy Banking in 2001; and **Kees van der Heijden**, for his work to develop the theory

I would like to thank the DTN team:
**Per Espen Stoknes**—for his insightful feedback, partnership in building a business, constant intellectual challenge and friendship
**Annika Varjonen** with **Visual Impact**—for her remarkable visuals that captured the content and spirit of the discussions, and her personal grace
**Harry Smittenberg**—for his sharp camera work
**Swe Thant, Jan van Baren** and **Gabrielle Ng**—DTN's home team, for their long days and hard nights with rewrites and editing to bring this material to publication

**Niall Murphy**, for insisting that the DTN is much more than a talk club

The **Rotterdam School of Management** for its support and the honor of being a Fellow; the **Ashridge Business School** for the honor of being a Visiting Professor; and to both for the opportunity to teach students who teach me discipline in communication

A special thanks also to **Nana Manojlovic**—not only for the great graphics and design that distinguish the look and feel of the book, but also for her patient attention to our needs and wishes

And **E** without whom nothing would be possible

RABOBANK
The FUTURE of ICT in BANKING
INTERNAL PERSPECTIVE
The VALUE of OUTSOURCING
Is MORE in the FLEXIBILITY of ACTION than in the COST-SAVINGS!
-2-5% COST-REDUCTION
BUT THEN we lose OUT IN THE amount of CONTROL!
ORGANISATIONAL CHANGES
CHANGES in the MARKET
We're proud of making NO MISTAKES!
RABOBANK
YEP. At SEVERAL TIMES THE COST, and TIME.
1 Making SYSTEMS THAT WORK
IT'S raining AGAIN.
COST-CONSCIOUSNESS
What if we were to find a DIFFERENT PERSPECTIVE to COST & VALUE?
we need to DELIVER MORE for LESS MONEY
DESIGN for QUALITY
What if there was MORE VALUE to be FOUND in THOROUGH EXPLOITATION?
QUALITY = FIT to PURPOSE
...but at what COST?
...AS DEFINED BY THE CUSTOMER!
¿WHO is the CUSTOMER?
RABOBANK NEDERL
LACK of DISCIPLINE & CLARITY in SPECIFICATION SETTING
FUZZY EXPECTATIONS
RABO
I WANT IT ALL! WHEN CAN I
GET IT?
UNDERSTANDING THE CUSTOMER
AND THE CONSUMER
RABOBANK END CUSTOMER
POTENTIALLY CONFLICTING
It's CRUCIAL in enabling us to SUCCEED!
No way can we please all all the TIME!

At the start, every team member was interviewed separately about what we felt were the uncertainties facing Rabobank Systeemrealisatie.

Chapter 1

# Introduction to scenario thinking

Scenario thinking, introduced in business by Shell Group Planning in the 1970s, has evolved as a powerful methodology for enabling organisations to structurally *anticipate* change and incorporate external uncertainty into the internal decision-making processes. Building scenarios is the process of qualitatively and quantitatively sifting, sorting and combining these possibilities into a few stories. These stories are:

- Focused—They must matter to the future of an organisation or a department.
- Plausible—They must describe futures that could reasonably happen in order for a high-level manager to base his/her day-to-day decisions on these scenarios.
- Coherent—They must have a logical storyline, and not be a random extrapolation of the plethora of trends with which managers are endlessly confronted.
- Surprising—They must challenge existing assumptions.

A good scenario set consists of two to four stories that all meet the above criteria to the same degree. The stories of the scenarios should not be focused on the developments that the organisation—in this case, Rabobank ICT—can influence. Instead, it should focus on the developments that it cannot. The question for Rabobank ICT is not to choose which scenario to realise, but to develop business ideas and options to respond to these different possibilities. *Scenarios create a language for talking about the future.*

Scenarios are not predictions; nor is it crucial for the scenarios to perfectly reflect the eventual future. What is important is that the scenarios challenge the organisation's managers and executives to become leaders. Scenarios sharpen their ability to act proactively to recognise, manage and take advantage of changes in their business environment. The scenario process is a tool for learning—not a predictive device. The process teaches us to learn from possible tomorrows in order to make more informed decisions today. The true value of scenarios are the strategic conversations that result from the scenario process, and the options generated by each of the business units based on the scenarios; not their predictability. The language that is created through a scenario process enables the organisational dialogue to operate with reference to many futures.

In this chapter I shall introduce scenario thinking, and briefly discuss the sequence that we adhered to in this process design. My intent is to describe the Rabobank scenario case history of Robabank ICT—not to give an exhaustive discussion of scenario thinking. I shall, however, illuminate some specific aspects that are relevant to this particular scenario process design, and how we approach scenario thinking at the DTN.

Much of the contemporary literature on scenario thinking focuses on a particular stepwise approach, with methodologies passionately espousing the benefits of a 10 versus 7-step approach. I believe that this debate is misdirected. In both our practice at the DTN and in my classes on scenario thinking, I oppose canonical adherence to one or the other of the methodologies. In practice, good scenarios are created using a range of different methodologies; and a good facilitator is able to familiarise himself or herself with the different approaches, mixing and matching them as appropriate for the particular situation, content and client. Every situation is particular. The intent of this book, therefore, is not to advocate a methodology, nor to propose a template that should be used. Rather, it is meant to demonstrate how a real-life scenario process unfolded: the participants, the thinking, the resulting scenarios, and some indication of the strategies. As the last element is company confidential, it will only be superficially treated in this text.

# Scenario & strategy process design

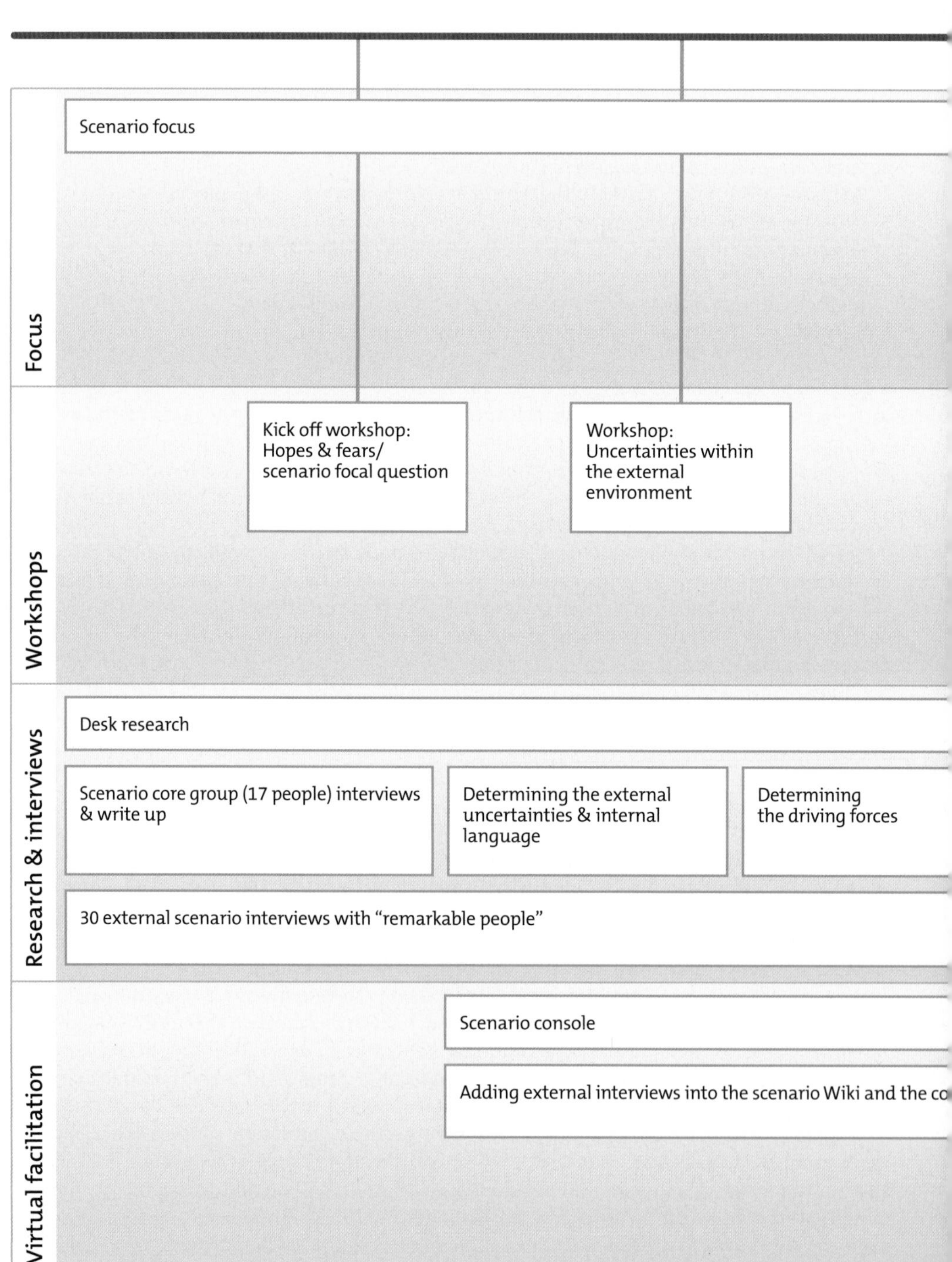
Focus
Scenario focus
Workshops
Kick off workshop: Hopes & fears/ scenario focal question
Workshop: Uncertainties within the external environment
Research & interviews
Desk research
Scenario core group (17 people) interviews & write up
Determining the external uncertainties & internal language
Determining the driving forces
30 external scenario interviews with "remarkable people"
Virtual facilitation
Scenario console
Adding external interviews into the scenario Wiki and the co

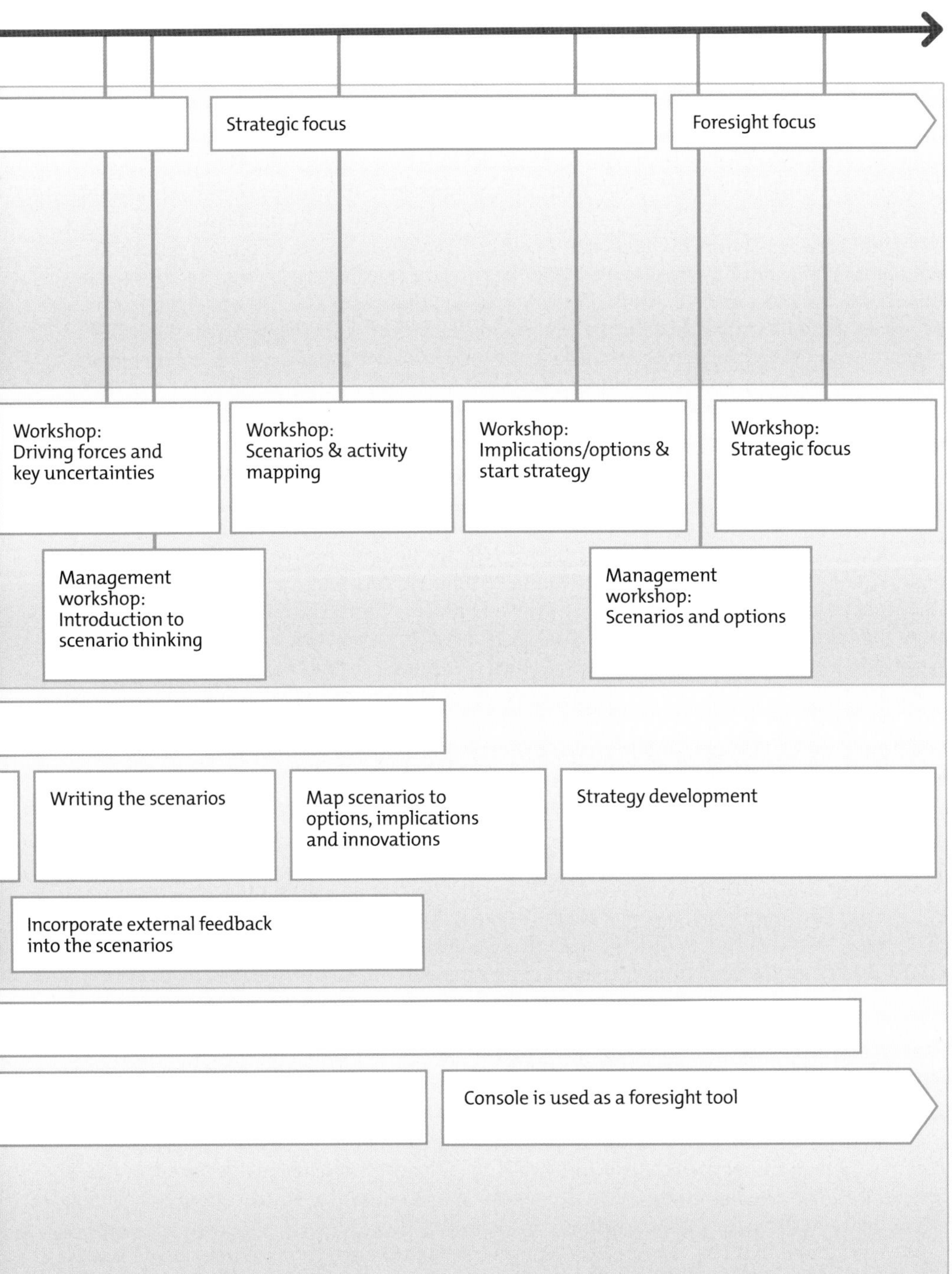
Strategic focus
Foresight focus
Workshop:
Driving forces and key uncertainties
Workshop:
Scenarios & activity mapping
Workshop:
Implications/options & start strategy
Workshop:
Strategic focus
Management workshop:
Introduction to scenario thinking
Management workshop:
Scenarios and options
Writing the scenarios
Map scenarios to options, implications and innovations
Strategy development
Incorporate external feedback into the scenarios
Console is used as a foresight tool

## Hunt gorillas

For more than 10 years I have been looking for a way to viscerally experience scenario thinking. Dr. Andreas Bluhm, who was head of exhibitions at the Van Gogh Museum at the time, introduced me to a fascinating exhibit at the Exploratorium in San Francisco. The exhibit is based on the research by Prof. Daniel Simons of the University of Illinois at Urbana-Champaign on what he has termed "inattentive blindness." The exhibit is a short video of people playing basketball. The viewer is instructed to count the number of bounces made by the members of one team. In the process of concentrating on the one thing, the viewer does not notice a large gorilla entering the frame, beating his chest, and then leaving! When I show this video, I ask the audience whether they "notice anything unusual?" To which, they respond by listing some important but mostly trivial aspects: "There is some graffiti on the wall," "There are a number of dummy passes," etc. On second viewing, the viewer is instructed not to count the bounces; and to our "shock and amazement" a giant gorilla walks through the scene! It is impossible to believe that this gorilla was in the original video. The initial reaction of audiences is that "it is a different video"—which it is not.

There is much to the world that we simply do not see. And decision making in our personal and organisational lives is based in part on an imagined reality, rather than on what is actually going on. The video reveals this at a visceral level rather than as an intellectual abstraction. How, then, do we manage organisations effectively, when we recognise that we are missing important events in the world? Scenario thinking can help.

This demonstration encapsulates the scenario process perfectly. We need to stand back from the routine of daily business, and ask ourselves, "Where might the gorillas be?" Then we go and hunt them. Scenario thinking is the structured process of standing back from our current instrumental tasks, bringing new voices and insights into the executive discussion, challenging ourselves to think through the implications of these new combinations of voices (possible futures), and responding to these challenges in innovative and creative ways. This is no simple task.

## Kill Buddha

"If you meet Buddha on the road, kill him!" The oft-quoted phrase from the 9th Century Zen master Lin Chi shocked me when I first heard it. After many months of puzzling over the phrase, I realised that learning comes from a journey. People who claim shortcuts sell empty promises. Scenario thinkers have a deep distrust of futurists, because they claim to know the future. Scenario thinking is not futurism. It is a learning process that makes the different tomorrows alive in the actions, innovations and imagination of executives today. Rather than claim that we can know the future, that it is something that can be studied as an object out there—which futurists often do—scenario thinking assumes that we cannot know the future.

Furthermore, research into trends, which are the stock of futurism, generally affirms the current mental map, rather than challenges its validity in the context of long-term uncertainties, or reveals blind spots. To hunt the gorillas, deeper thinking is needed, a journey through the jungle is required, and curiosity is a precondition.

We have found that scenario projects typically last about a year—sometimes even longer—to facilitate a natural rhythm between the day-to-day business, and a proper block of time to think about tomorrow's tomorrow. However, many of the long-term insights are already applied in the daily business throughout the scenario process, rather than sequentially. The Rabobank ICT process took a little over a year, which all the participants felt was a good pace for the process.

At the DTN we often state that there is no past and no future. Both are constructed from the present. Therefore, we cannot study the future (or the past for that matter) in an objective way—we are studying the present, and our perceptions of both. Scenario thinking is the structured process of bringing possible future events into the decision making of today. This process would be much less valuable if the organisation or team were to be informed of a single future, as if tomorrow could be known as an extrapolation of today's trends, by a "guru" who claims to know the path ahead. If you see him, kill him.

## The future is plural—not official

Most executives never discuss the future. They are concerned with the complexity of managing today. On the odd occasion that executives have a chance to reflect, the futures they describe tend to be set and unchanging. This is because there is a future that people in the organisation implicitly ascribe to: scenario thinkers call this the "official future."

The official future embodies all the small assumptions that people in the organisation share and never discuss, and therefore, never question. For example, the official future for most telecommunications companies today is that the cost of communication will continue to depend on distance and time.

Scenarios always challenge an organisation's "official future." They show that the official future is only one of several, and that other possibilities are equally plausible. Executives therefore need to plan for the entire spectrum of possible futures. In the case of telecommunications, these might range from a "free global communication" future to a future of "pay-for-service-not-reach."

In questioning the official assumption, executives start to discuss the future with greater sophistication. External developments are viewed as indicators of a particular scenario. These developments are debated and continually compared with the assumptions of their effects in the different scenarios.

Thinking about tomorrow is therefore richer if we accept the need to think of the future as a plural. The future cannot be predicted as a singular reality, waiting to be discovered or deciphered. The future is uncertain. Since the beginning of the 20th Century hard sciences have questioned the existence of an objective, knowable reality in the present, not to mention the future. What we call "the future" is characterized by change, and the uncertainties, surprises and shifting dynamics created by changes taking place elsewhere in interconnected fields: social, political, ethical, technological, etc. Therefore, scenario thinking differs from forecasting the future to imagining multiple futures. It also dismisses the assumption that the changing and complex dynamics in the interaction between people and the circumstances around them can be predicted with mathematical accuracy. Although scenario thinking uses both quantitative and qualitative data in discussion and analyses, it refrains from imposing statistical certainty or predictability on future plausibility. All scenarios are equally likely.

## Brighter than a thousand heretics

Pierre Wack, who introduced scenario planning into the commercial context at Shell and famously anticipated the first and second oil crises, advocated the need for organisations to cultivate a network of a thousand heretics: people who do not mind questioning the established truth, but who like to think with open curiosity about the world. These are the people who look at the world and have a slightly different way of thinking about the causal relationships that shape our reality. In the later, more politically correct years, this network of people has been called "remarkable people"—a beautiful term—by Kees van der Heijden. In my best definition, I would describe them as people who leave you thinking about the world in a different way each time you have a long conversation with them. It is as if the world had shifted in the conversation. These are the people we go to learn from to realise a scenario project. This network is one of the most valuable assets one can bring to a scenario process. Without these individuals to graciously give us their time and insights, this scenario project would not be possible. The interviews are conducted as scenario-style semistructured sessions, in which we explore the aspects an interviewee does not know, rather than the long list of trends. We try to capture the "delicate futures," the seeds of potential futures, that are not yet discussed or codified. When looking at the word, one tends to forget that every powerful technology, social dynamic or institution—from computers to capitalism, from the European Union to the Grand China Project—was once a fragile idea. It is these ideas that we look for, for they contain the seeds of the futures that will surprise us, and hence, challenge our strategy.

During this particular scenario process for Robobank ICT we interviewed 30 people on three continents, each for more than two hours. It is a specific style of unstructured interview that leaves both the interviewee and the interviewer exhausted. As a hard rule, each member of the management team participated in at least one interview. This is important, because it brings executives into new and unfamiliar spaces, conceptually and physically. It also places an executive in a situation where he or she has to listen and not judge, which is different from the normal organisational regimen. The 67 hours of interviews, conducted on three continents, have been organised into 575 themes, transcribed into just over 300 pages, and edited into 40 hours of video.

One often learns as much outside the formal interview situation as one does in the interview itself. I recall eating sushi at the Blowfish in San Francisco, in the middle of the dot-com slump, and everybody assumed that real ICT was moving to India with, perhaps, some ideas being developed in the Valley. Eating the surprising combinations that one would only be able to find in California, we concluded that the defining characteristic of California is its ability to reinvent itself. It is a bottom-up process that is embedded in the fabric of the social space. Eating delicious, strange sushi, unrecognisable to a Japanese traditionalist, we concluded that the term "Web 2.0," just coined, had substance. ICT is not just technology; it is philosophy. It is the way people think about complex systems—a premise that all ICT magazines keep getting wrong. ICT in the Bay Area had just reinvented itself, and the deeper question was not when ICT was moving to India, but *how these two centres of innovation and expertise would relate to each other.*

## It is the shared language, stupid!

Why make ICT scenarios or an ICT strategy? Organisational strategy today is inseparable from information and communication technology (ICT). Only through linking managerial and technological perspectives can we build strategies that have business value and technological relevance.

Unfortunately, most organisations are not prepared for the new technologies that have the power to transform them. Why? Consider the following dialogue:

Q: How will we serve our high-value customers better when they are on the move?

A: Well, when our Seibel implementation is done we shall have an end-to-end CRM solution. The question is how we link this data set into an integrated mobile service offering that is secure, and give access to key transaction parameters.

The problem is that most managers do not have a clue what ICT professionals are talking about, and ICT people cannot explain their work in management-speak. The technical lexicon used by ICT professionals is needed to talk about the topic in depth. But, it is inaccessible to others. ICT professionals and management are two sociological groupings that speak different languages. Consequently, conversations between the two are limited in scope and give rise to little learning. This discursive divide is responsible for many of the day-to-day ICT problems that plague the process of information management.

Scenario thinking is a powerful method for bridging the divide. It links thinking about business and technological changes into a conversational framework in which managers and ICT professionals can learn together instead of talking past each other.

Scenarios move the conversation from the present to the future. In creating scenarios, therefore, ICT professionals have to talk about the effects of technologies and not just about the technologies themselves.

Scenario thinking is an open, exploratory process. Building scenarios is not a matter of filling in the blanks, but a process of creating new, distinct images that describe future worlds. Today's assumptions—embedded in the day-to-day conversations of managers and technicians—do not suffice to capture tomorrow's complexity. The scenario-building process thus forces participants to create a new language that is adequate for the new situation. When both technical and nontechnical people take part in this process, they share the new language, which is neither technical nor managerial, but combines both types of discourse.

## Bitter medicine works the best

The best-laid plans of mice and men often go awry, to paraphrase Robert Burns in his poem *To a Mouse*, after turning up the winter nest of a mouse on his farm. This is more true of organisations than it is of mice. The purpose of a scenario process is to challenge decision makers in the organisation with timelines that lead to a failure of their current plans. This has two consequences.

First, the key participants in the scenario process should have decision-making authority over the strategic scenario space. The scenario team should then predominantly be line managers: people who feel the problem in their gut; people who would sleep better if they knew the future of this specific question. It is their enthusiasm and drive that continually refocuses the scenario question. And from the start of the scenario process these executives and managers can apply the key external insights into the daily business. Many scenario processes have failed to produce the expected business value because they have been approached from an exclusively staff perspective. The staff are then consequently in the questionable position of advocating significant changes in the plans of their line executives.

Second, good scenario sets have a bite to them. As a rule of thumb, I like one of the scenarios in the set to challenge the fundamental business idea of the organisation. This is not a simple matter, and for this reason the lead facilitator of the scenario process should never be an internal employee; nor should the executives respond to the scenarios at the end of the process. It is an interactive learning process, and as in auditing, scenarios are best made through a combination of internal and external insights. Combining internal decision-making authority with well-researched, deep external challenges in a structured learning process is the only way that I have discovered scenario thinking can lead to the breakthrough strategic decisions that it has the potential for generating.

## Know nothing, learn everything

To emphasise: scenario thinking is a learning process. To demonstrate this seemingly trivial statement I would like to relate a "tale of two scenario sets" developed at roughly the same period of time for two clients:

- **Scenario set # 1**
  "Once you have made them we shall workshop the scenarios. We do not have the time to step back from our daily business for a learning process". This seems a reasonable inclination, but it risks compromising the scenario process."

  A significant failing in our professional practice at the DTN was a scenario process which we facilitated for another client in 2000. Due to time pressure, we delivered the scenarios with a shallow learning process, in which the executives had minimal involvement in the creation of the scenarios themselves.

  At the final presentation we informed the CTO and the executives that their investment of three-quarters of a billion Euros in next-generation infrastructure would not be successful. For the executives, it was easier to reject the challenge of the scenarios than face the consequences of their past decisions. The scenarios were seen as a political threat rather than an opportunity to shift their mindset into the new challenging futures. Although threatening on the surface, these futures presented significant new business opportunities. Even though the scenarios accurately anticipated all the key developments in this industry sector for the next five years, the organisation did not act on the scenarios. They were filed and forgotten— a significant strategic opportunity was lost and, two years later, the organisation was at the mercy of its creditors as it was dealing with a very different business environment.
- **Scenario set # 2**
  Concurrently with the above, we were developing a set of scenarios for another organisation. This involved a learning process, including a set of workshops, interviews and reflections. At the end of the process the executives found themselves in a very different strategic context, as they were confronted with the post 9/11 situation and a 20% budget cut across the organisation.

Uniquely in this larger situation, the department, for which we developed the scenario set, was able to defend its budget and argue for a strategic acquisition between € 30–40 million. Six years later the organisation sold this acquisition for just under € 400 million.

The key difference between the two scenario cases is not the substantive financial benefit that was accrued in the second scenario set, but that the executives had internalised the strategic challenges. This learning enabled them to argue a compelling and counterintuitive business case in a challenging environment. One does not know something unless one has learnt it.

## Memory of the future

The Swedish neurobiologist Prof. David Ingvar coined the term "The Memory of the Future" in a similarly titled article in *Human Neurobiology* in 1985. He explored the classical tripartite concept of time (past/present/future) and postulated that our sense of the present is informed by both past and future memories. The concept is that we have action plans that are being formed based on the constant development of alternative "multiple time paths into the future." It is as if we are making a memory of the future to make sense of the complex sensory input in the perceived present. The implications of this research and the proposed model is that at a neurobiological level we are all scenario thinkers.

We make scenarios all the time. We are charting different paths or constructing "alternative time paths into the future." For example: "If I finish work before seven I can stop by the green grocer's. But if I don't I can try the night shop." Having thought about these contingencies, we are prepared to act. Tapping into this natural tendency to construct and internalise alternative options for acting in the future, scenario thinking generates learning that enables institutional decision makers to anticipate and to respond adeptly to new business conditions.

Scenario thinking therefore works in organisations because it builds a "memory of possible futures" in the executives' minds, and enables the organisational language to discuss these futures. It engages participants in activities that expand their perspectives and encourage new ways of looking at things in order to become more insightful about the changing world around them.

# Scenario cycle

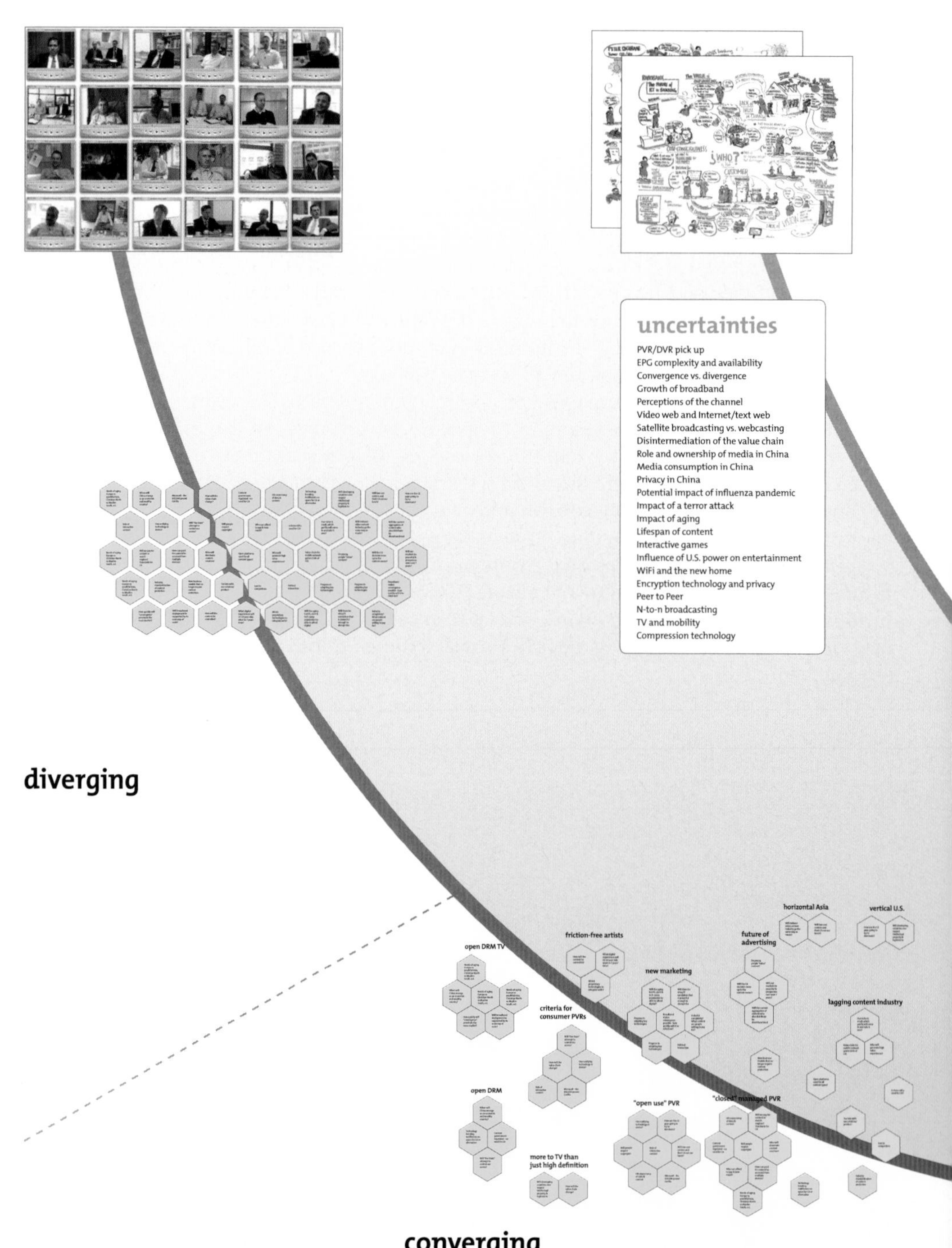

uncertainties
PVR/DVR pick up
EPG complexity and availability
Convergence vs. divergence
Growth of broadband
Perceptions of the channel
Video web and Internet/text web
Satellite broadcasting vs. webcasting
Disintermediation of the value chain
Role and ownership of media in China
Media consumption in China
Privacy in China
Potential impact of influenza pandemic
Impact of a terror attack
Impact of aging
Lifespan of content
Interactive games
Influence of U.S. power on entertainment
WiFi and the new home
Encryption technology and privacy
Peer to Peer
N-to-n broadcasting
TV and mobility
Compression technology
diverging
open DRM TV
friction-free artists
horizontal Asia
vertical U.S.
future of advertising
new marketing
criteria for consumer PVRs
lagging content industry
open DRM
"open use" PVR
"closed" managed PVR
more to TV than just high definition
converging

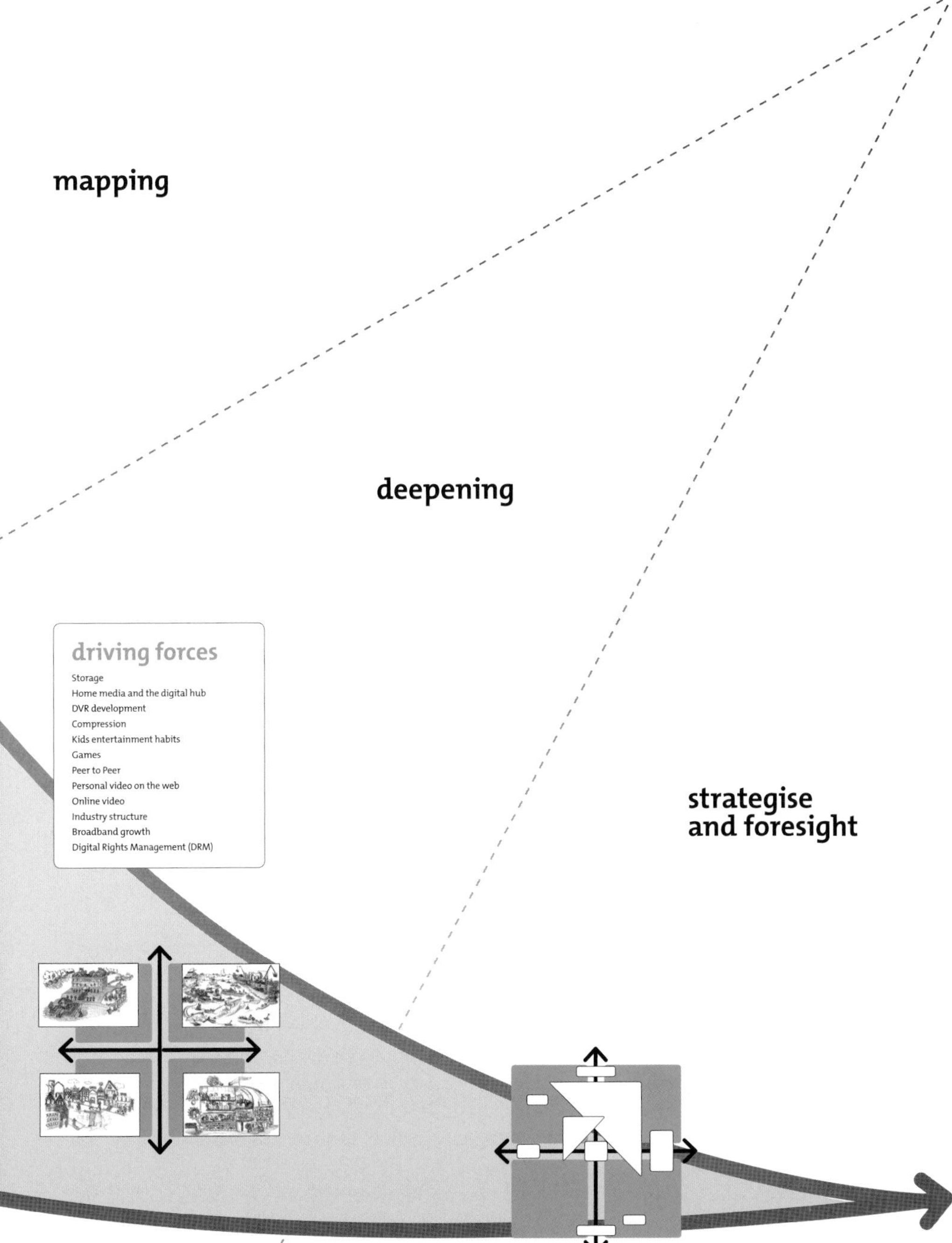
mapping
deepening
strategise and foresight
driving forces
Storage
Home media and the digital hub
DVR development
Compression
Kids entertainment habits
Games
Peer to Peer
Personal video on the web
Online video
Industry structure
Broadband growth
Digital Rights Management (DRM)

## The structure and elements of scenario thinking

Our scenario process, which covered one year of creating the scenarios followed by half a year of working on the strategy, consisted of specific steps that give structure and punctuation to the process. Without them, the undertaking would be a loose set of conversations about possible futures. The process takes place in workshops, and in internal and external consultations with experts. The final outcome are scenarios suggesting different possibilities and challenges. The following is a short outline of the process and the organising elements.

## Determining the focal question

In order to determine the focal question we interviewed the management team of Systeemrealisatie and key people in Rabobank Group ICT. These interviews were transcribed, thematically organised and visualized to represent and to create an understanding of how Rabobank Systeemrealisatie conceives itself and its strategic context.

Based upon this understanding we asked ourselves, "What is the key question we would like to answer about the future that would enable the organisation to function at a different strategic level?" In other words, we had to articulate the focal issue or decision that the scenarios are to illuminate. Scenarios are most relevant when they address a particular aspect of the future. That aspect should be a major issue or decision that the organisation faces. The focal scenario question that emerged after a day's workshop was: *What is the role of ICT in financial institutions in 2017?*

## Assessing the uncertainties

The protean nature of change makes for a world of chance, contingency and randomness. Thus, the next workshop, which takes place after two months, is devoted to exploring and assessing the elements that are uncertain but can be potentially influential to the topic or issue at hand. We examine known facts and plausible trends, identifying what is predictable or constant, and what is changing and uncertain over the time horizon of a scenario planning period. This examination is a fundamental exercise in building the logic for the scenarios. The key here is not to prioritise or pick key uncertainties, but rather to map the strategic space. It is from a conversation of this map that we start developing the scenario discussion. Executives start to explore implications of social, economic, technical, environmental and political changes.

The Rabobank ICT team discussed 22 uncertainties, represented by developments such as outsourcing, banking consolidation, a European payments market, emergence of nontraditional service providers, mobile banking, visualisation technology and demographic changes. The chapter on Uncertainties (see Chapter 4) gives a selection of these factors and the questions and challenges they raise; for example, questions about the impact of factors, such as local brand loyalty, the competitive advantage of proprietary customer information enjoyed by local banks, and the trend toward banking consolidation. Or questions may be about the changing labour markets and changing business needs that impose a new uncertainty on outsourcing and its rationale for businesses. Discoveries from other fields—such as social demographics that show changing patterns of consumption, wealth deployment, technology use in financial decisions, and what people look for in job searches—are examined for their potential to shape future banking services and their delivery mechanisms.

An example of the workshop discussions is summarized in the following excerpt from the Uncertainties workshop report: "ICT was thought of as a maturing industry with nowhere to go. However, a clear line that is arising from the interviews is that the financial industry appears to be at a tipping point, which has the potential to change the industry, similar to what the music industry has experienced before. Many opportunities may be found for those with the insight to look for them."

## External consultations (interviews)

Generally, people in organisations rarely seek experts from other fields or sectors to lend perspective on an issue. Scenario thinking stresses the importance of hearing from external experts who are outside the company's sphere of influence; individuals who have no interest in the company but are engaged, instead, by the ideas that are being explored in the scenario process. These interviews are a necessary part of the process to identify the driving forces that form the bases of the scenarios. Simultaneously, their ideas, insights and perspectives are expected to broaden the thinking of the scenario participants and to prompt them to think in new directions and uncommon ways.

These are the "remarkable people," individuals who are prominent in their fields. They are selected not only for their expertise in their specific sector, but also for their trenchant perspectives, their critical and unorthodox views, and the creative insights they bring to the discussion. For the Rabobank process, 30 experts from around the world were interviewed. These interviews are described in some detail in Chapter 6, the penultimate chapter of this book. of this book.

## Understanding the driving forces

Expert interviews give us a wide-ranging, multidisciplinary understanding of the scenario topic. Based on these consultations and broader desk research, the scenario group identifies a number of critical influences or driving forces behind the uncertainties in the landscape. This gives us a sense of the deeper forces that are shaping our strategic space. These forces interact with one another to create patterns of events that are often called "trends." In scenario thinking these driving forces are recognised as factors beyond our control or influence, but for which we can anticipate and prepare. From the uncertainties that had been identified, the Rabobank team drew a list of driving forces shaping the future of ICT in banking.

It is worth pointing out that some of the critical influences that were recognised—in some cases given identity—in the Rabobank scenario process, have in fact shown up in the current state of financial markets, and in the "sea change" that is occurring in the architecture and delivery of computing services. Recognising developments, such as the potential for peak oil, and the decline of the dollar, led the team to suggest a major shake-up in world financial markets. Forces such as Web 2.0 with its collective power of small sites, user contributions, delivery of software and continuous innovation; flat-layered computing, a term we have given to large-scale clusters of massively parallel computing systems using inexpensive hardware and small computers; and mashups, can be seen in the emerging wave of changes that could offer a compelling alternative to propriety applications and services. A selection of these factors is described in some detail in the chapter on Driving Forces (see Chapter 5).

# Scenarios and strategy

Scenario processes combine outside-in and inside-out thinking to produce new strategic thinking. The scenarios are developed to describe possible future worlds outside the organisation's direct area of influence (contextual environment). Subsequently, the complex processes internal to the organisation that produce strategic value are investigated. Finally, these two insights are combined to produce a coherent picture, which I call a Scenario Map. This map enables executive teams to match their strategy to external uncertainty and visualise if a strategy is unbalanced—biased to a specific scenario—and visualise which part of the strategy is robust and which part of the strategy is contingent. An example Scenario Map is illustrated on the next page (29).

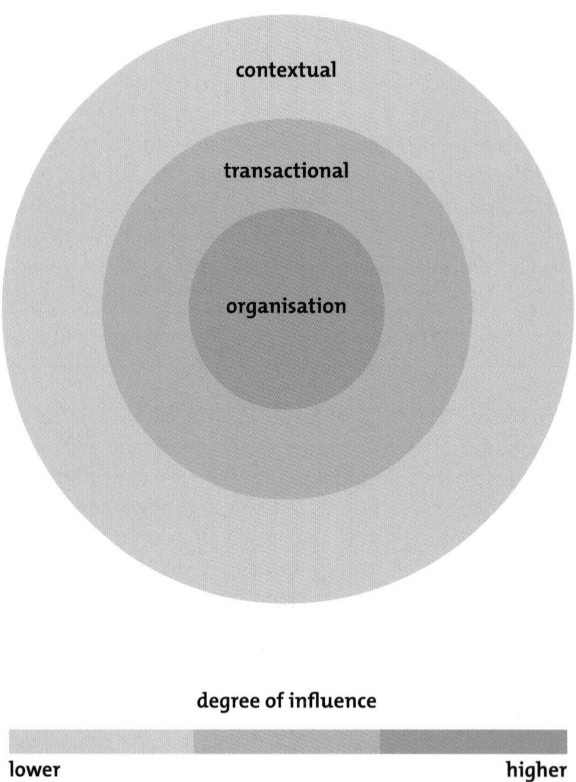

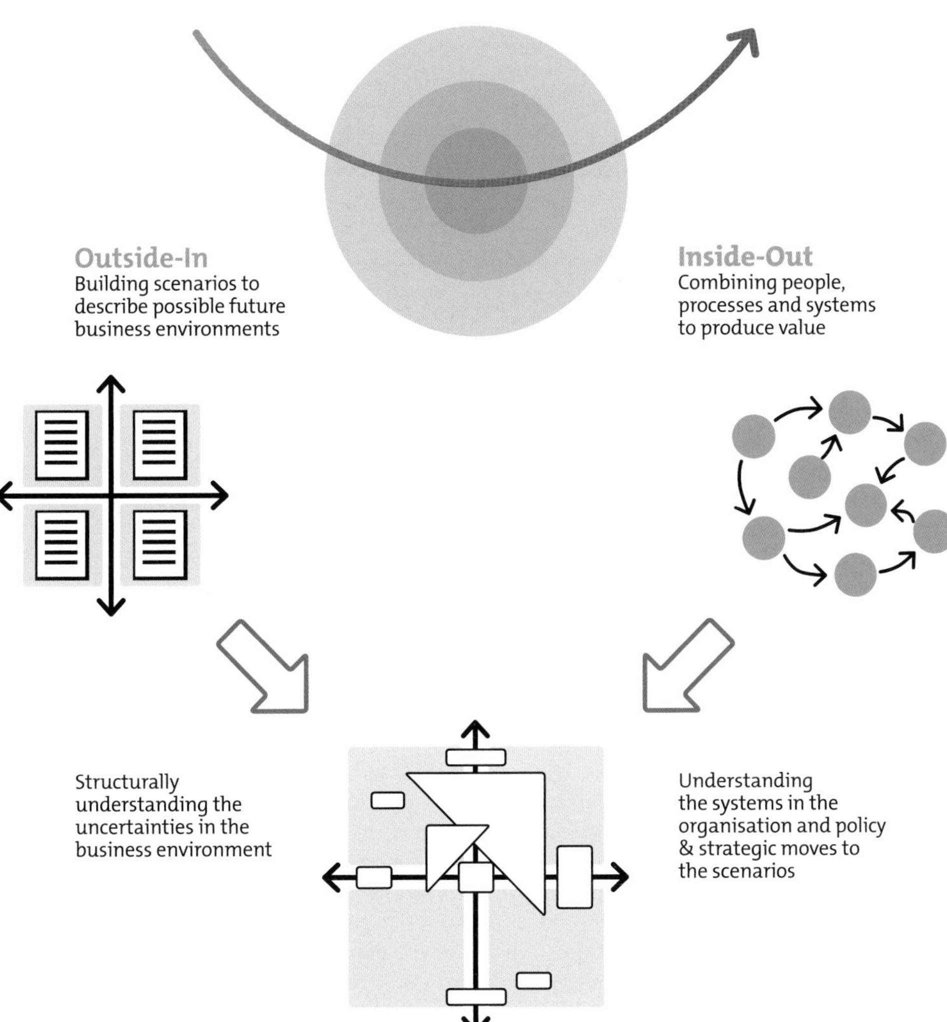
Outside-In
Building scenarios to describe possible future business environments
Inside-Out
Combining people, processes and systems to produce value
Structurally understanding the uncertainties in the business environment
Understanding the systems in the organisation and policy & strategic moves to the scenarios

## Determining the uncertainties

In our third workshop that took place over two long days, we reviewed all the interviews, desk research and driving forces to decide which scenario stories about the future would be told to the organisation. If we want to describe the role of ICT in financial services in 2017, what stories are important to know? Or stated slightly differently: how can we create stories that challenge our strategy best?

Generally, the key uncertainties are determined using an impact/uncertainty matrix on which the team maps the driving forces. It is my experience, however, that this process often leads to rather predictable scenarios that do not challenge the organisation sufficiently. At the DTN we often make systems-thinking diagrams, combining all the driving forces in natural language systems, clustering like ideas and phrases. From these diagrams, we "read" the scenarios. In this case we spent half a day discussing possible scenarios in preparation for converging on our four scenarios. It is the lowest point in the process as the participants are challenged to keep the entire content of the process up to that point in their conscious mind. At this point "it is simply too much," and the team naturally switches from a divergent to a convergent process. After selecting the scenarios, the team experiences euphoria.

It is important to note that this is a messy process. The neat decision tree that describes the scenarios in the scenario chapter was determined after the fact. It is a communication tool that aids our explanation of how the scenarios could emerge, rather than as a thinking tool as it is often presented.

## Crafting the scenario stories

Based on the uncertainties and the driving forces, the participants develop a set of (four) scenarios, each describing a possible future and its environment. Developing the scenarios is itself a journey of thinking through the causality of possible scenarios themselves, a process of recognising different situations that can happen, instead of one specific set of things happening in the world. The scenarios are not options from which the company will choose one as the most likely, or choose one as its preferred future in which the company can decide to operate. Rather, the scenarios raise different possibilities. All are plausible, all are situations that can happen, and all are outside the influence of the company to control.

Scenario stories are not written in a single session, but are written and rewritten. In this case we rewrote the scenarios seven times; each time, changing a causal sequence here, bringing an insight from the interviews there, etc. A good scenario set strikes the difficult balance between surprise and plausibility. Only if a scenario is surprising will it introduce new elements into the strategic space; and only if it is plausible will executives respond strategically to the new challenge.

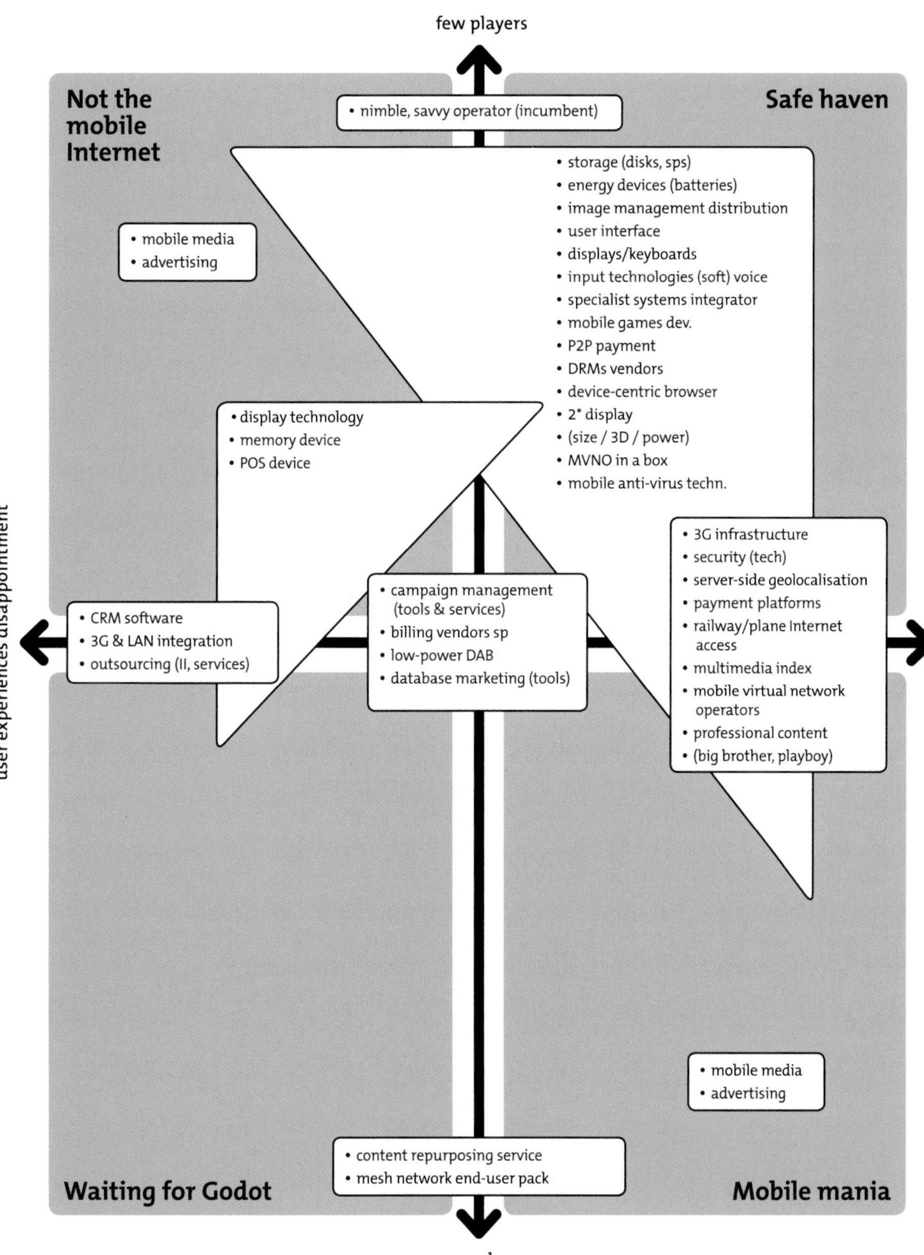


Scenario map of investment opportunities in the mobile Internet in 2007 made during industry workshops in 2002

## Strategy and foresight

Our strategy was developed in four succeeding workshops, and is an ongoing process. Unlike the scenarios, the strategy is seen as confidential and treated superficially in this text in the postscript.

We have an ongoing foresight process in ICT Systeemrealisatie where we provide support for thinking in scenarios. These two activities are as follows:

- **Observing early warning signals**
  Using a specially devised, collaborative intelligence gathering tool called the ScenarioConsole, the team observes new events. These events are automatically mapped to the scenarios, and additional themes, that the team has chosen, and are tracked. This sophisticated foresight tool helps the team to monitor a scenario that is more likely to occur through sentiment analysis.
- **Updating the scenarios**
  Each year the team performs 10 additional interviews that are brought back into workshops to keep the scenarios and scenario thinking current in the organisation. We thus have an ongoing scenario-thinking process that continually challenges our current thinking about possible futures.

## Broadening the net

The uncomfortable reality for most executives is that they are not really in control of the organisation. At any moment, thousands of decisions are made in the organisation, many of them with significant strategic implications, and much of it outside the executives' sphere of influence. Organisations are run by people, from the top-down and from the bottom-up. It is therefore important that the scenario stories become a broadly used tool throughout the organisation, both at an ontological and an epistemological level. Ontologically, because it presents a way of thinking about the world—not in a way limited to the assumptions of an “official future”; but an expansive future, rife with possibilities that should be thought and often planned through. Epistemologically, because the scenario stories present coherent frameworks for thinking about external events and of how to respond to them.

The scenarios have been presented to the Rabobank Group ICT. In ICT Systeemrealisatie we developed a card game based on the scenario content that can be used in workshops and as a thinking/creativity tool. This book, and the videos on the dedicated wiki, also function as channels for bringing the scenario stories into the hearts and minds of the broader organisation.

For me the Systeemrealisatie Management Team only really started with the first workshop in the scenario process. In those two days we laid the foundation for the team's mentality: the impossible exists, but time always brings change. Anyone who takes this into account knows that nothing is impossible.

Jos Mijnen

Chapter 2

# Rabobank Group: A brief history

Rabobank Group comprises one of the world's largest financial institutions and is distinguished by its AAA international credit rating from Moody's and Standard & Poor's. Founded on cooperative principles, its historical roots are deeply entrenched in the agricultural community and the local loan cooperatives that were established in the Netherlands nearly 110 years ago by entrepreneurs with little or no access to capital. The first agricultural cooperative bank was founded by a German rural mayor, Friedrich Wilhelm Raiffeisen. Having witnessed the poverty suffered by some members of the farming community, Raiffeisen first set up a charity to provide financial relief. In 1864, Raiffeisen transformed the charity into a cooperative bank, having determined that lasting improvements were more likely to be achieved through self-help rather than through charity.

In the late 1890s, the German cooperative movement spurred the establishment of agricultural cooperative banks in the Netherlands. Generally founded by local notables, such as clerics, mayors, philanthropists and wealthy farmers seeking to aid peers who were less fortunate, the cooperative banking system subscribed solidly to pragmatic business principles. These "practical pillars of an idealistic philosophy" included:

- Unlimited liability of its members;
- Unpaid management;
- Profits reserved for further growth;
- A field of operation limited to the local area; and
- Association with a cooperative bank, while still retaining local independence.

The banks prospered; and one of the leading factors in their success was their mode of operations at the local level. Local member banks established offices at the heart of the local community. Their proximity to customers meant that the banks knew their clients personally. This competitive advantage allowed cooperative banks to become adept at selecting creditworthy farmers and to closely supervise their loans. The end result was the ability of these banks to provide agricultural community loans with better interest rates while simultaneously building and retaining a loyal customer base.

Rabobank today is the merger of two central cooperative banks: the Centrale Coöperatieve Raiffeisen-Bank of Utrecht, and the Coöperatieve Centrale Boerenleenbank of Eindhoven. Both were founded in 1898 and were fundamentally different with respect to geography, and to political and religious affiliations, reflecting the diversity between north and south Netherlands. The bank from Utrecht was fundamentally Protestant, and the Eindhoven bank was intrinsically Catholic. Furthermore, the Centrale Coöperative Raiffeisen-Bank supported local autonomy while the Coöperatieve Centrale Boerenleenbank held a more stringent and centralized organisational structure.

The two cooperative banks merged in 1972, driven by three primary influences:

- An increase in the number of offices, which created competition at the local level;
- The fading of denominational dividing lines in the Netherlands, which diminished the importance of ideological differences that divided Utrecht and Eindhoven; and
- The widespread merger trend in the Netherlands, creating a greater demand for capital in the business community, which in turn promoted consolidation in the banking sector.

The newly merged bank was called the Coöperatieve Central Raiffeisen-Boerenleenbank, and became known generally as "Rabobank" from the first two letters of the original names, Ra and Bo.

Eventually, the bank adopted this shortened form and legally became Rabobank Nederland in 1980.

Today, Rabobank Nederland is the central organisation of the Rabobank Group, consisting of 183 local independent Rabobanks, which are in turn members and shareholders of Rabobank Nederland. While it provides full financial services, the institution operates on cooperative principles, distinguishing itself by two of its chief characteristics: it maintains a long-term view, and retains its historical concern for the role of the bank in the community and its contribution to society.

In its decision to engage in a scenario-thinking process with the DTN, Rabobank recognised an emerging need seen among financial institutions. The speed and complexity of changes in the market have placed demands on traditional institutions to look at new imperatives for doing business and to develop effective strategies in response—or risk being eclipsed by rivals. As an initial step to strengthen Rabobank's continued presence in the Dutch financial sector and to ensure its strong emergence in the global financial industry, Rabobank decided to leverage the power of scenario thinking to examine the future of information and communication technology in banking.

At some point in the first workshop the assignment was to think of a scenario where Rabobank would go bankrupt. The reactions went from "that is impossible" to enthusiasm for the exercise. But at the end of the first workshop, it was this discussion that laid the base for an attitude of not being religious about what is possible and what is not.

Jos Mijnen

Chapter 3

# The scenario stories

The Rabobank-DTN scenario process was a year-long journey, undertaken by a small group of dedicated managers from the bank and scenario specialists from the DTN. The departure point for the process is always the formulation of the scenario question, and the remainder of the scenario process is dedicated to answering this question. After a full debate, the Rabobank team unanimously agreed on the question: What is the future of ICT in banking in 2017?

Over the course of the year, core team members traveled to diverse locations around the world to consult with leading experts. The full team engaged in an iterative process of reviewing the ideas and insights presented by the experts, and participated in workshops and discussions about the key uncertainties and the driving forces in the future of ICT in banking. The process culminated in the development of four scenarios, which reflect a core principle of the process: thinking across multiple futures to anticipate for the surprises, and the challenges that emerge with change. The scenarios presented below were meticulously crafted by the bank's team members.

# Future role of ICT in financial services in 2017?

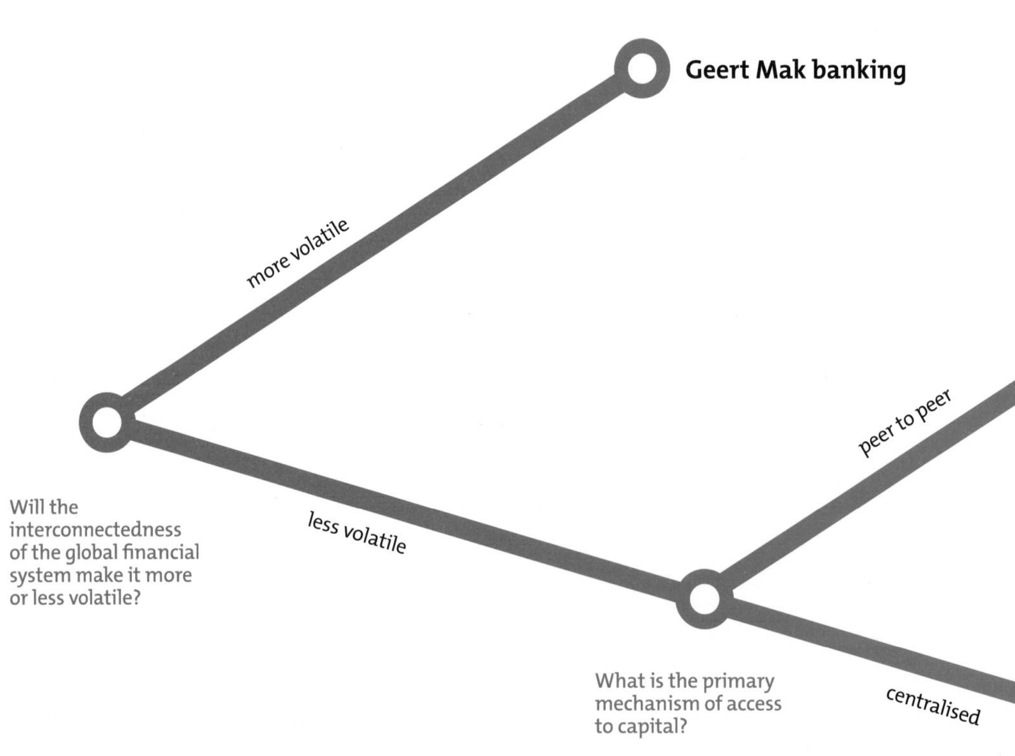

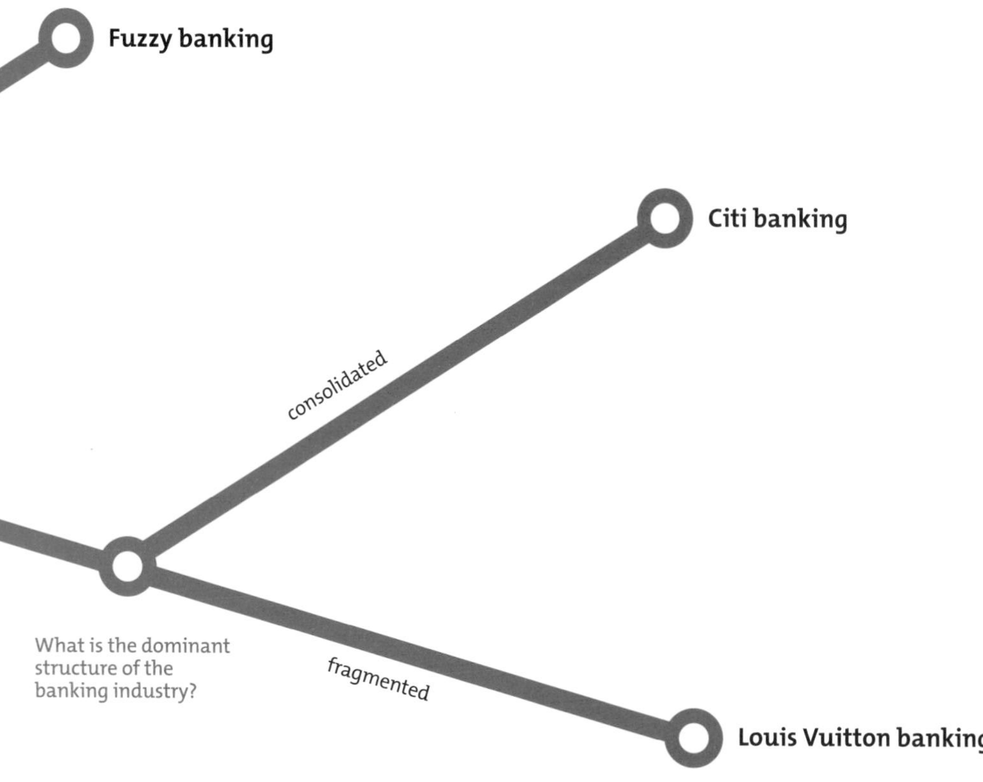
Fuzzy banking
Citi banking
consolidated
What is the dominant structure of the banking industry?
fragmented
Louis Vuitton banking

# Fuzzy banking

This world is a world of overinformation. Flooded with a multitude of financial offers, customers switch providers quickly and easily, searching for the best deals. New service providers emerge that mediate transactions between investors and bank offers, using eBay-like web interfaces. In a market of mass investors and many small providers, open source banking is the de facto form of banking transactions. Under this system, the customer's identity is his or her most valuable asset.

## 2007–2008

With the economy recovering in 2007,
customers were increasingly swamped with
a barrage of new service offerings from different financial institutions. Feeling over-
whelmed by the onslaught, most customers
postponed making decisions, choosing not
to deal with the chaos. Banks could not
understand the lack of customer response to
their attractive new offerings, and unleashed
flashier marketing campaigns and even more
products, thereby increasing the confusion!
In their frustration, many customers began
to think about changing financial services
p115 providers.

The Dutch finance.google.nl (beta) was
U11 D3 launched in 2008, and was very successful.
The value-added feature of finance.google.nl
was the way it leveraged Google technology.
Users entered search criteria, such as risk
U8 D8.3 rating, duration of investment, sector, etc.
In response, the search engine returned
relevant information and investment
opportunities. Search history was saved on
the user's personal account page. The fact
that the API was open and that the licence
encouraged other providers to offer services
D10 on top of this interface attracted little notice.
Mortgage companies were one of the few
financial services providers to take advantage
of this development.

## 2009–2010

The excitement of the Beijing Olympics the
previous year carried over into 2009, and
further bolstered globalisation and global
economic growth. The coming of a new D6
U.S. president into the White House in 2009
revived hope for a more stable international
political and economic climate, giving people
confidence to try new things. New initiatives popped up everywhere. Web interfaces
were set up by small companies to mediate between the banks and the customer,
offering the products of any bank. Improved U6 U10
visualisation technologies helped to make
sense of the range of available products and
services. At the time, financial institutions U7 D4
did not perceive these small initiatives as
a threat and barely reacted to it. They were
more preoccupied with fancy new products
to adapt to an accelerating market of ever-
changing customers.

Open software offered a solution for creating many new products, since it was a cheap
base for new software development, and suf-
ficiently flexible to allow for innovation. This U11 D3 p138 p244
effectively redefined the role of ICT into one
that needed to build on top of open source
software and its many capabilities to create
combinations that seemed to add the most
value.

Legend:

Ux Uncertainties chapter, paragraph number; page 87–95
Dx Driving forces chapter, paragraph number; page 97–109
px page number in the Interviews chapter; page 113–269

## 2011–2012

Trying to deal with all the new products, more and more customers experimented with the new interfaces exemplified by finance.google.nl. eBay's strategy was to p143 buy the interface with the most potential.• eBay then developed this interface into eBay Finance, which was launched at the end of 2011. As is done in its marketplace, eBay's Finance site served as an intermediary, connecting individual investors and small-U11 D3 scale investment projects.• The success of this initiative drew on the trust generated by its existing PayPal brand, and trust from the feedback and rating system adapted from eBay's marketplace.

Seeing the growing success of these new web-based financial service models, banks began to show concern about weakening U6 customer loyalty.• They realised that simply launching new products would not help customer retention. Their answer was to start developing their CRM systems that actively and intelligently reacted to customers' financial activities. This enabled customised services or "geared to you" services for the masses.

## 2013–2014

The completion of the International Space Station (ISS) several years ago resonated as a moment of accomplishment for people worldwide. For the Boomer generation, this was the culmination of Space Age exploration, which rose to its height during their youth.• This event sparked renewed interest U13 D2.1 in space exploration. Feeling young and reinvigorated, they were ready for new frontiers.• Seeing the success of the eBay/Google p129 financial service models, they felt confident enough to invest their considerable savings through these channels.

Recognising the flood of money in the market, many entrepreneurs, all wanting a piece of the pie, started new specialised web initiatives to attract Boomer investments.• p267 Primarily, experienced Gen-X dot.com veterans managed these initiatives, which were the brainchildren of the Millennials.• This U14 D2.2 meant a higher possibility of success based upon the past experiences of Gen-Xers who had gone through the dot.com bust of 2001. The repercussion of successful new entrants into the market was loss of market share for traditional banks.• U4 p199 p214

Many new customers were young, successful professionals who treated finance and investment as a game.• Banking within p232 cyberworlds, such as Second Life's game world, provided customers with fun, novel and engaging user interfaces.

## 2015–2016

With the introduction of a new kind of computing into mainstream software applications, a whole new approach to information technology became possible. Financed by Boomer investments, innovation surged. Successful projects revolutionised technologies, such as avatars and voice recognition.* p158 U7 New opportunities for web applications were explored with the increasing efficiency of information streams on preexisting bandwidths.

Investors saw the potential of the new initiatives and looked for investment opportunities. The increasing number of investors and innovators created a highly competitive investor market for the projects. The new wave of investments took place through the intermediary service model. As a result, banks became marginalised as service providers.* p196 Some blended their activities with their own mediation services, while others essentially became channels for money flow. Both investors and innovators were customers of the intermediary service providers, while also remaining as providers of funds and investment opportunities. Effectively, the line distinguishing customers from providers became blurred.

Although banks had become marginalised as service providers, they had a distinct advantage in their new primary role as service intermediaries. The development of a secure banking desktop eliminated the need for many IDs and passwords to access the sites of each separate financial service provider. Through the bank's single secure system, customers needed only one single password in order to access all their preferred financial services providers.

In the increasingly competitive market, smaller providers needed to pool their resources together, cooperating with one another in larger projects that generated more revenue.* p115 Existing groups, small and medium-sized enterprises and student fraternities, took some of these cooperative initiatives. Some soon became an economic force to be reckoned with, leading them to regain a lot of their lost splendour.

## 2017

In 2017, the financial market was a highly complex sector in an extremely dynamic and highly innovative society. The industry was fluid and fast-moving, composed of many small service providers and some larger ones functioning within a multilayered structure.* D9 Traditional financial institutions could be found here and there, but they had largely blended in with their surroundings, the most successful being those who were compelled to shed their old features and had quickly adapted at an early stage.

With the new banking model, old regulations for the financial sector became obsolete, necessitating new rules. Regulatory debates, especially about how tight the new rules would be, caused friction in the European parliament. However, this had little impact on the market, since Europe's role was greatly diminished by the fragmentation of the global market. It was also difficult to implement new regulations because of rapid changes in the market.

The combination of financial service offers, and the convenience of switching providers. meant that customers could change providers at their whim. This new "throwaway" culture is dependent on whatever appeals to customers at any particular moment.

The image of Fuzzy banking is one of a Thai river market—a complete chaos of people, boats and merchandise if you look at it from a distance. But if you come closer and study some of its details, it turns out that there is not so much an order in the chaos, but a fluent logic that makes it all work unbelievably efficiently. It is a logic that the most thorough research could never completely work out. No one has a complete overview, but the larger players in

the luxury liner have some overview. Smaller players of various sizes and abilities try to put together small deals.

The role of ICT, as represented by the actors in orange, is to keep the market flowing by solving little problems in the system and to keep the general flow of goods efficient and fast by making sure channels remain open.

# Scenario characteristics

## Cooperation
Investment opportunities will be made available for the masses, and not only for private investors. Anyone can take up a service request. As a result, the market will be highly competitive. At the same time cooperation will be crucial, since small players will have to depend on one another for larger projects.

## Structure of financial services
financial services will be fluid and fast-moving. There will be many small entities and some larger institutions, providing services to customers within a multilayered sectoral structure. Banks will become mediators of financial services. These services will be offered by individual entities within networks, some of which may be less familiar—such as the eBay market of buyers and sellers—than others, such as the Corps, an economic fraternity, where members invest in each other and where membership is managed for exclusivity, giving more power to Corps members.

## Outsourcing
In this context outsourcing will lose its meaning. Because of the fragmented structure of the market, it could be argued that everything will be outsourced.

## Global financial health (economy)
The health of the global financial market/ economy will rely upon bottom-up technology acceleration. This acceleration will be driven by a wave of new technology and broad access to investment funds that had not been available before.

## Demographic perception
The Boomer generation will hit retirement. Not only does this income group have money to spare for investments, but it also has a willingness to invest. The Millennials, managed by the experienced Generation X dot. com veterans, will provide consumption and entrepreneurial drive to ensure the success of Boomer investments.

## Regulations
The economy will be more open, having been deregulated. Under this open banking scenario, individual investors will be directly linked to individual investment offers. Since it is a new banking model, old regulations for the financial sector will no longer apply.

## Globalisation
The globalisation process will continue to gain momentum and accelerate as a response to increased innovation worldwide: being innovative will be more important than being in the right place.

## Interface technology
Taking advantage of the benefits of mashup approaches, banking providers will work to reduce interface complexity by creating new mashups that aid the evaluation of deals and mediate trust. (The pieces can be witnessed in eBay's seller evaluation and ownership of PayPal.) Visualisation technology will be paramount in making sense of the plethora of offers.

## Physical interface
Apart from the eBay-like interfaces on the web for the channeling of investment by the masses, there will be some investment opportunities for private investors through salon investor circles. Face-to-face encounters are always better for mediating trust. Many investment communities will emerge as a result of this.

## Web technology
Banking parties, web technology will be based on mashups, and they will provide secure systems to mediate trust. One key enabler would be the further development of identification technology for enhanced security.

### Back-end technology
Open standards will dominate the technical space. The use of open source and open standards would be in line with the culture of the Millennials, who are more open and accepting of open innovation in their approaches.

### Open source
Open banking will become the de facto form of banking transactions; old bank labels will remain, but essentially become the "eBay for banking," providing referral services. The key success criteria will be the ability to generate and elicit trust.

### Europe
In this scenario, Europe will hardly play a role in the banking world: borders will have no function in this fragmented market and regulations will rarely apply.

### Customer demand
Banking services will be included among specific products and services, as we already see with cars and home technology. Therefore, the provision of banking services will basically be a good deal that will go unnoticed as a separate service.

### Role of ICT
Since a major part of the technology is open source, the role of ICT will be to enable collaboration among different developers in this open infrastructure. Another role will be to take the offerings of open source software and to build on them, developing combinations that add value.

### Private banking services
Private banking services will be commoditised and democratised, with better differentiated investments. This will enable custom services or "geared-to-you" services, rendering private banking services irrelevant.

### Retail banking services
Retail banking services will be stripped to its barest level: a debit and/or credit card. Identity mediation is what adds value to the retail banking area.

### Wholesale banking services
The bank will become part of an investment community, effectively using the same technologies and approaches, but on a lesser scale. These services are oriented around deals and will be much more transparent, implying that they will be less profitable in the future.

### SME banking
Traditionally underfinanced, this area will experience the greatest growth. Investment clubs will be based on "peer-to-peer" concepts, perhaps tied to industry sectors or other affiliations (e.g., Fair Trade investors network). As a result, there will be many small investment communities.

### Complexity reduction
The complexity in this scenario comes from emergent phenomena, similar to the 1987 stock market crash when automated trading systems caused the crash and led to the introduction of stock gaps to freeze trading. The corresponding challenge will be to anticipate and mitigate for sudden and unexpected changes.

### CRM
This area must show new development, and will be driven by the individual. In this scenario, there will be a move from a push- to a pull-system as a result of too much information (e.g., Google AdSense).

### Culture
A throwaway culture will exist in this world of fast and fluid services.

### Trust
A trust in the system and its mechanisms will exist in this scenario, similar to the kind exhibited by eBay, where members have trust in eBay interrelationships.

### Client identity
The identity of the client will be his/her most valuable asset, not dissimilar to the value of eBay feedback and rating.

### Loan
Loans will be granted based on product and trust rating, which may be something that emerges similar to a (decentralised) credit history, or even product history.

### Bank budgets
Bank budgets will allocate funds for open innovation. How will financial institutions find new products and insight in trading, creativity or a winning combination that is able to combine things in better ways (e.g., Google AdSense linkages)? Innovation will be more focused on combining things versus creating things. Pushing advisory, rating and community services will be a large part of bank budgets.

# Citi banking

Banks are consolidating across borders into much larger entities. The increased capacity allows these large megabanks to bring product and ICT development under their own roofs. Banks are thus able to efficiently offer a full range of services to customers. Sophisticated technological developments reduce the need to maintain many branches and a large human workforce. This is leaving banks with the problem of putting a "human" face on large-scale proprietary ICT systems.

## 2007–2008

Despite persistent unrest in the Middle East, the global economy was booming in 2007, D6 and markets continued to integrate. In the financial sector, banks were working hard to adapt their ICT infrastructure to new European requirements, such as Basel II, the Single European Payments Area (SEPA) and U3 D5.1 D5.2 D5.3 the Lisbon Agenda. Rising compliance costs as well as uncertainty of required future skills made the integration process even more complicated.

In order to alleviate the associated difficulties with complying with the upcoming deadlines of the new European requirements, the financial sector used software packages provided by such vendors as SAP and Oracle/ Siebel, which became the basic building p170 p179 blocks in this environment. These packages standardised processes and helped to minimise associated compliance costs in the changing market environment. Software that was specific to banking processes, however, was developed and maintained in-house.

Although banks across the entire financial sector were uncertain as to what specific new skill sets would be needed in the near future, larger banks, with more resources and greater access to people with the right skills, were relatively better equipped to comply with these new requirements. Smaller banks experienced more problems with the integration process, on both fronts. Banks in general sensed more complications in the future with the approaching deadlines of other requirements.

The adoption of standardised software packages led to the increased harmonisation of ICT systems across the entire financial sector, U2 p250 paving the way for sector consolidation.

## 2009–2010

In the time leading up to the 2009 European Parliament elections, the general feeling about Europe became more positive as people felt more involved in the creation of a single Europe. There was also evidence of greater acceptance of the cross-border entry of "foreign" European banks. Customers could access and transfer money anywhere within the EU-2 with greater ease. This change was widely noticed and appreciated.

As the deadline for SEPA approached, the requirements for new ICT skills became even clearer. However, banks still had great difficulty finding people with the right skills for the implementation of new European banking requirements. Smaller banks, more so than larger banks, increasingly experienced problems keeping to the compliance schedule. Bigger banks struggled as well, but because of their scale, they were able to cushion a lot of their problems.

The deadline for SEPA came into effect in 2010. Some banks were unable to develop their ICT systems to comply with new SEPA requirements on time. p237 These banks were unable to effectively compete, making them easy prey for hostile takeovers.

Across the sector, small and big banks alike observed that bigger was better. Following the logic of economies of scale, more and more banks started to approach each other to discuss mergers. p261 Now that systems were more harmonised, inter-European mergers were far simpler. In addition, the Capital Requirements Directive (CRD) for Basel II removed barriers to cross-border mergers and acquisitions. Furthermore, the financial sector leveraged the earlier experiences of national bank mergers and intra-European bank mergers. Some of the smaller banks looked for opportunities to cooperate across the border, rather than choosing to merge with another bank.

Legend:

Ux Uncertainties chapter, paragraph number; page 87–95

Dx Driving forces chapter, paragraph number; page 97–109

px page number in the Interviews chapter; page 113–269

## 2011–2012

The Freedom Tower, built upon the site of the former World Trade Centre and completed in 2011, was a harbinger of the belief that bigger is better.

The harmonisation process of ICT systems across the financial sector to comply with new European regulations was long, arduous and complicated. However, as the wrinkles began to be ironed out, the possibility of mergers became more and more attractive for banks. Larger institutions had the resources to offer a full range of products to customers and the scale to support these services with large-scale monolithic ICT systems.

Since most of the new ICT skills were not available at home, only part of the development process was kept in-house, while most of it was outsourced to India and other countries around the world.• U1 D7 Rather than dealing with the complexity of working with many service providers and managing the outsourcing process, large banks maintained their own captive centres, leveraging price and labour differentials in developing countries.• p219

## 2013–2014

As the consolidation process gained momentum in the financial sector, news about new bank mergers seemed to feature more frequently.• U2 Such financial services providers as mortgage and insurance companies merged with bank brands under a single umbrella of financial services. European megabanks began to appear. These new banking entities had to quickly find a way to provide reliable and uninterrupted service to their amalgamated customers.• p121 The increase in scale became the primary complexity that the financial sector had to contend with. This was largely the responsibility of ICT development. Factors contributing to this complexity were harmonisation of systems of the merged partners, resolution of residual problems with implementing SEPA, and setting up processes to efficiently deal with millions of customers.• p127

Bank budgets appropriated more funds for ICT departments, which needed more and more money to keep things running efficiently and smoothly.• p149 Capital expenditures also included the purchase of innovative technologies developed by external technological firms.• p175 These purchases helped banks to pursue innovation while keeping internal ICT research and development costs down.

## 2015–2016

Having rebuilt most of their ICT systems to accommodate their expanded size, banks were now running on predominantly self-developed, large-scale, closed systems. These systems had the potential to provide customers with a customised full-service offering from all merged partners. ICT efforts were now focused on developing proc-
p177 esses to support this.* Internally, the new megabanks began large-scale reorganisation efforts, while preparing a massive rebranding marketing campaign.

Unable to efficiently deal with millions of customers, banks adapted their CRM systems, steering clients into specific categories
p239 for greater efficiency.* Customers were either assigned an identification number by their banks or used a preexisting number, such as a sofi or passport number. Despite this necessary robotic approach, on the front end, banks tried to give clients a sense of person-
p263 alised attention.*

The first marketing efforts were launched by the end of 2016. The new bank brands were revealed and marketed the significant advantages of one-stop shopping.

## 2017

As marketing campaigns continued, more customers signed up for packaged services, seeing the advantage of having all financial services under one roof. Not only was there a reduction in the inconvenience of managing multiple financial services and products from multiple providers, but there were other advantages from recent ICT developments. A major advantage of these megabanks was that ICT developments had been able to cut the costs of private banking services to make them available for the masses.

Because of the inconvenience of physically visiting bank branches, customers increasingly addressed banking needs via the web.* U6 U10 p256
Thus, the workforce within physical banks branches was drastically cut down. A nominal human workforce was retained for complicated service requests and tasks.

However, some customers continued to feel alienated from their banks. Despite the successful use of technology across the financial sector, the remaining challenge for financial services providers was to put a "human" face on large-scale monolithic ICT systems. Subsequently, avatars and other rich interface technologies played a key role in this development.* U7 D4 p169 p195 p243

A global oligopoly financial market was the final result of consolidation and globalisation.

The image of Citi banking is one of a huge factory, where everything and everyone is geared to efficiency and where every customer can get exactly the product he or she wants,, as long as it is the product the bank provides. Customers, like everything else, are a uniform product that needs to be processed as efficiently as possible. It would be most desirable to replace them with robots. The core function of customer relations, digitalised as much as possible, is to keep

customers away from the bank, while keeping them satisfied at the same time.

The role of ICT, as represented by the actors in orange, is a major one. ICT basically runs the machinery of the bank on every level. Keeping systems running, matching the systems of new acquired banks, customer relations, are all part of ICT. But nearly all of it is commoditised and outsourced, keeping only a few maintenance functions in the bank itself.

# Scenario characteristics

## Cooperation

Because of globalisation, the consolidation of the financial sector will be widespread. There will be only a few major players, and almost no smaller players, having been absorbed into the larger entities. This will result in a global oligopoly financial market.

## Structure of financial services

Since the bank is a large entity, it will have the capability to provide all services to all customers. There will be no need for a customer to go elsewhere for more specialised services. Some products will be loss-making for the benefit of being a full-service financial institution.

## Outsourcing

Banks will have their own captive centres in India and elsewhere, and will thus have no need to outsource services to third-party players.

## Global financial health (economy)

The WTO Doha rounds will succeed, creating a smooth economic space. Scope is everything. The global economy will be stable as a result of managed integration across geographic sectors. Large multinationals will exploit price differentials in labour and resources in the North-South, East-West. Consumer confidence will be high.

## Demographic perception

The financial sector will leverage the investment confidence of the Boomer generation, who will place their savings and investment decisions in large institutions (e.g., blue chip, transnationals) with whom there is a pre-existing and established relationship. A new generation will follow this trend.

## Regulations

The regulation framework will enable and even encourage consolidation of the financial sector because of the detailed regulations that only large players can live up to.

## Globalisation

As consolidation extends across borders, globalisation will accelerate as a result and vice versa.

## Interface technology

The challenge for financial institutions will be to put a "human" face on large-scale monolithic ICT systems. Monolithic systems are the only way to serve customers, but how can customers leverage the full-service offering? Avatars and other rich interface technologies will play a key role in this scenario.

## Physical interface

Banks will have few but large city branches that are heavily dependent on technology in service as well as security, with a marked emphasis on process management. Routine services will be largely done by avatars, while for complicated tasks, employees will still be available.

## Web technology

Banks will run on predominantly self-developed, large-scale, closed systems that provide full service. There is no need to go to the branches anymore, since any contact can go through the web as well.

## Back-end technology

The financial sector will develop most back-end technology itself, outsourcing parts of the development to their own captive centres. They will create and maintain full-service provision packages.

## Open source

The software that is used by the banks will not be open source at all. Existing open source solutions might be used on their own non-open systems when they are useful, but this will be strictly limited to cherry-picking, if it happens at all.

### Europe
The merging of the European markets will go on and will be successfully completed. In the end, Europe will operate as a single market.

### Customer demand
The customer demands convenience above all else, which will be met by package deals, full-service branches and highly developed web technology.

### Role of ICT
The role of ICT in this scenario will be to develop software that ensures efficiency and scale in the front- as well as in the back-end technology. Additionally, ICT will enable mass customisation. financial services will be delivered as a lot-size of one.

### Private banking services
Mainly through technological innovation, the labour intensity of private banking will be reduced drastically, making it available for mass customisation.

### Retail banking services
The key activity of retail banking services will be to use technology in an advisory capacity, guiding the choices of the customer in situations where single large scale products must be accommodated to customer need.

### Wholesale banking services
Wholesale banking services will become larger in scale.

### SME banking
This will not be seen as a valuable sector, and will effectively be retail banking.

### Complexity reduction
In this scenario, scale is the primary complexity that financial institutions must contend with. The challenge will be to manage the complexity of scale. As stated by Jaron Lanier, software beyond a certain complexity becomes unmanageable.

### CRM
CRM in this scenario is a push-system, implying that process management will be crucial to direct flow. Financial institutions will be unable to deal with 10 million customers, or do it efficiently, and must therefore steer customers into categories. Anticipation of potential flows will be a key success factor.

### Culture
This world is one in which efficiency rules. Risk management will be prominent.

### Trust
Customers will place their trust in the institution or the brand.

### Client identity
Clients will be reduced to numbers to their financial services providers.

### Loan
Loans will be granted based on credit history and underlying assets. The entire loan process will be conducted through intermediaries.

### Bank budgets
Bank budgets will place an emphasis on efficiency, process improvement, acquisition, organisational streamlining, operational excellence, and advertising. Part of bank budgets will also be allocated for the development of a few large-scale new products.

# Geert Mak banking

The world is recovering from a global financial crisis brought on by the bird flu pandemic. Money is scarce in the market, and the investment climate is highly risk-averse. Financial institutions need to adapt and be able to do more with less. Rebuilding customer trust in the system is a primary consideration. Foreign satellite branches are sold off as banks bring the focus inward, returning "home" to country-level oligopoly markets.

## 2007–2008

Dozens of bird flu-related deaths in Indonesia in a single month in 2007 touched off a new wave of fear and panic all over the world. By the end of the year, the bird flu virus, having mutated into a human-to-human strain, had arrived in Europe. Soon afterwards, similar cases were reported in the U.S. Although the number of casualties worldwide was on the side of the optimistic scenarios, the impact on the global economy was devastating. Investments decreased dramatically as did domestic trade, now that consumers all over the world remained at home as a precaution. Many people were ill and unable to work. The situation in the U.S., which was still recovering from Hurricane Katrina, was especially dire because many families and businesses were already heavily in debt. U.S. consumers
D1.1 were soon out of money.*

These events lead to a dramatic drop in demand on the global market, affecting every single country in the world, with Asia receiving the heaviest blow.

The 2008 summer Olympics in Beijing welcomed far fewer fans than previous Olympic events had. The Games were more popular than ever, however, because many more viewers tuned in from home.

By the end of 2008, while recovering from the flu pandemic, the world was in a deep recession, and globalisation had come to a grinding halt with countries looking inward
D1.4 D6 to save their own economies first.* What remained was an extremely risk-averse climate. The focus of ICT departments of most companies, especially banks, was to quickly develop stable and secure systems to ensure
p121 the continuity of operations.*

## 2009–2010

On the brink of collapse, companies pressured national governments to protect their interests. In reaction to this and the need to protect the interests of the labour force, some governments mobilised themselves to prepare to freeze the liberalisation process of the market.

Defaults on bank loans and mortgages, which were traditionally high revenue earners, resulted in significant stress on bank coffers. Banks and mortgage companies alike suffered losses, and the general availability of money in the market was limited.

As a result of the economic depression, customers held on tightly to their money. Short of putting it into a sock, they demanded safety and security from any
financial institution.* Customers preferred U8
bank products and services, such as savings accounts, which were low revenue generators. Investments were generally seen as too risky by oversensitive customers, who wanted to remain as liquid as possible.

The 2010 FIFA World Cup in South Africa welcomed a record number of fans. Recovering from the crisis, the world found an opportunity to celebrate through this worldwide event.

Legend:
Ux Uncertainties chapter, paragraph number; page 87–95
Dx Driving forces chapter, paragraph number; page 97–109
px page number in the Interviews chapter; page 113–269

## 2011–2012

At the start of 2011, the dust clouds of the pandemic finally started to blow over. What appeared was a less complex world, pulled back into small regions. Unofficially, Europe was now a conglomerate of countries. National governments continued to abide by EU legislation, but did not seek to work further for a more united and borderless Europe. Money was scarce because of continuing low levels of consumerism and investment activities. The major challenge for the banks, as a result, was to do more for customers with p219 fewer resources.*

Most banks had set up an even more secure system on top of preexisting systems that met customer demand for security. This included improving identification and anti-hacker technologies. ICT departments needed to retain a large workforce to support the continued maintenance of legacy p225 systems.* Outsourcing was minimised or U1 D7 rejected entirely.* For some banks, everything was developed and maintained in-house. Others chose to offshore processes to other countries, but still within Europe, such as to Poland.

People showed strong nationalistic feelings at the 2012 summer Olympics in London, reflecting the continued protectionist attitude of national economies.

Meanwhile, transnational banks, which had started to consolidate just before the flu hit, could not handle further complexity of U2 their widespread organisations.* Combined with new protectionist legislation and a shortage of capital, the consolidation process effectively came to a halt. As a result, a country-level oligopoly started to take shape.

## 2013–2014

Things had calmed down enough by 2013 to look into the future. People were coming to grips with lower living standards. For the last few years, people had been very cautious with their money, gradually replenishing their savings accounts. They were more optimistic towards the future, and were tentatively expressing some interest in investing in low-risk initiatives. However, customers continued to demand safety and security above all other requirements. Thus, a significant amount of bank budgets was spent to maintain or obtain better A ratings.* p263

Part of bank budgets was also allocated for innovation. Small, incremental improvements were made to both front- and back-end systems, but banks chose not to risk making any radical changes. Their goal was to provide uninterrupted and reliable service to give customers a strong sense of security.* p184

## 2015–2016

By 2015, a large part of the Boomer generation had already entered retirement.* U13 D2.1 Family ties had become more important during the crisis. Boomers in general abstained from investing in an unstable financial market. However, they were strong supporters of their children, often using their money to back them up in major purchases, such as home mortgages and entrepreneurial efforts. Family-run small and medium-sized enterprises (SMEs), backed by Boomer money, started to become one of the most important customer segments.

Banks increasingly integrated mortgages into their financial services offerings. Boomers were looking at second mortgages and Millennials were beginning to consider purchasing their first homes.* U14 D2.2 Customers tended to stay with their preferred banks, with whom there was an established and preexisting relationship.* p205 Banks that could also offer mortgage services added value to their customer relationships.

## 2017

The situation in the financial market was a clear and quiet one. Although national economies were showing initial signs of recovery, partly based on SMEs, there was no indication that the globalisation process would accelerate in the near future.

Customers preferred to come into the branches for face-to-face transactions.* p232 p205 Private rooms replaced counters in the local branches to create a more intimate atmosphere. In these private rooms, each visiting customer could be met personally by their personal account manager or, in rare cases, a specialist for specific services.

On the ICT side, things were much the same as before the pandemic, but with more emphasis on reliability and safety. Simple transactions could be done online through a direct connection with the bank's closed-system network. Visualisation technologies were leveraged here to help people realise and resolve problems on their own, adding value because people felt more in control of their finances in an uncertain world.* U7 D4 p226

The image of Geert Mak banking is one of back to the good old days of the '50s, when we were safe in our houses, people were polite and could be trusted, and banks were solid institutions, like Fort Knox, that knew best how to keep your money safe. In these days, things were simple. We were proud of our country and our national institutions. No complicated mortgage schemes, no banks trying to lure us into loans that we don't really need and may not be

able to pay for, and we had some distance from untrustworthy, unbalanced foreign financial systems that could threaten our safety and integrity.

The role of ICT, as represented by the actors in orange, is plumbing. Their function is to make things run smoothly, to keep things hygienic without being noticed. The only way they would be noticed is when they are not there. No creativity or innovation is required.

# Scenario characteristics

## Cooperation
The process of consolidation of the financial sector will reverse, meaning that a country-level oligopoly market will re-emerge.

## Structure of financial services
financial services will be traditional, meaning that every service can be negotiated because there is almost constant contact with the customer. For example, mortgages will be negotiated from a base offer.

## Outsourcing
The financial sector will outsource almost all ICT services. Although the perception would be to do things closer to home, needed skill sets will not be there.

## Global financial health (economy)
Because of some kind of major global crisis, consumerism and investment will decrease dramatically. As a result of this blow, the global economy will effectively come to a halt.

## Demographic perception
The Boomer generation, despite havng significant savings upon retirement, are reluctant to make investments in an unhealthy financial market. The Boomers will "hold on to what they have," a trend that will be followed by succeeding generations.

## Regulations
Regulatory liberalisation will reverse, and the architecture will be set up to provide local protection against foreign competition.

## Globalisation
As a result of the global crisis and the following collapse of the global economy, the globalisation process will stagnate. The result will be an even more separated world.

## Interface technology
Interface technology will be the same as now, meaning that it will support basic services. Tradition, reliability, safety and security will be key.

## Physical interface
Counters will be replaced by private rooms for visiting customers to meet each personally for their individual needs. A large part of the customer contact will be done at the home of the customer.

## Web technology
Banks will run closed web systems. These systems will not be sophisticated, and will only cover basic services.

## Back-end technology
Banks will rely more heavily on software packages from third-party vendors. This reliance will imply less innovation, as specialised packages will come from a few suppliers.

## Open source
Since security of software has top priority, open source will hardly be used in this scenario.

## Europe
Europe can be described as a conglomerate of countries or regions, working together in some fields. In this scenario, each country or region will be more inward-focused. Europe will be seen as a cluster of entities.

## Customer demand
Safety and security will be the top concerns for customers. In investments, for example, they will prefer to choose low-risk investments rather than high-risk, high-profit ones.

## Role of ICT
The ICT department's role will be to ensure that the bank has stable and secure systems to maintain the continuity of operations.

### Private banking services
These services will be provided exclusively for high-net-worth clients.

### Retail banking services
An account manager will be assigned to each customer account, in a paternalistic approach to banking services. Transactions will not necessarily be completed at the bank's physical location, as emphasis will be placed more on remote transactions.

### Wholesale banking services
Since there will be far less money around as a result of the crisis, less capital will be required. Wholesale banking services will be smaller, resulting in national-based syndication.

### SME banking
Small and medium-sized enterprises will be recognised as being an important customer segment. Banks will take a paternalistic and supportive role, to help them with their financial decisions.

### Complexity reduction
Complexity will be low. Everything will be straightforward and simple in the financial world. The main challenge will be doing more with less.

### CRM
CRM will not be important and will be handled by humans, not by software.

### Culture
The predominant culture will be very risk-averse.

### Trust
For the customer, the bank will be represented by the account manager. Trust in the account manager as a person will equal trust in the bank.

### Customer identity
The way customers are perceived by financial institutions will depend on their personal and family history with the institution.

### Loans
The possibilities to get a loan will depend on the underlying personal assets of the customer and on his/her family assets.

### Bank budgets
Bank budgets will be allocated for the consolidation of one payments and savings system that is designed to be trustworthy and for the long term. Since the client will come to the bank, not much will be spent on marketing. A significant part of bank budgets will be spent on obtaining or keeping triple-A ratings.

# Louis Vuitton banking

To stay in the game with fickle and trendy customers, successful market players quicken their responses to ever-changing fads. Financial service provision spreads to a set of different specialised providers who begin to offer financial services on top of white-labeled and multi-labeled business processes. Banking services and products, which are available everywhere and are subject to trends, are geared more than ever to lifestyles and less to traditional customer segmentation metrics. New entrants, unencumbered by legacy systems and behaviour, significantly erode margins on financial products.

## 2007–2008

The steady growth of the European economy in 2007 fortified confidence in the future. Surveys showed that consumer confidence was getting stronger all over Europe. As a result, the market for lifestyle goods and services grew beyond expectations, while customers became used to being served their every need and whim.[p127, p163]

In financial services, sustainable banking brands, which took responsibility for the impact of their activities on society and the environment, were growing fast. They met the lifestyle of an increasing number of customers who followed the trend of sustainable consumerism.

Consolidation of the financial sector continued at the national and European levels in anticipation of the Single European Payments Area (SEPA).[U2, U3, D5.3] The implementation of the Capital Requirements Directive (CRD), a Basel II directive to remove barriers to cross-border mergers and acquisitions within Europe, paved the way for future intra-European consolidation.[D5.1]

The strength of the euro, combined with the growth of the European economy, strengthened international confidence in Europe's role in the international arena of major economies. These developments encouraged non-EU banks to consider introducing financial services into the Euro-zone. The deregulation of the financial sector created a "borderless" Europe. The lowering of traditional market barriers opened up the European financial sector to new entrants, other than non-EU banks.[U4] Rather than focus on national preferences, they specialised in specific lifestyles.

## 2009–2010

The completion of the Virgin Galactic Spaceport potentially opened up the field of space tourism. This attainment of a generation's dream represented the belief that anything is possible. This was reflected in indulgent customers demanding personalised services to meet every aspect of their lifestyles.

The idea that banking services should meet people's lifestyles spread beyond sustainability. Customer demands increased by the day, even as the customers resisted paying more and became increasingly inclined to change financial services providers. In order to meet those demands, financial services providers looked for solutions to change their systems and reduce costs.

Most financial services providers turned to outsourcing as the best short-term solution to increasing service and reducing costs. They prepared to outsource nearly all of their ICT departments, only keeping some specialised ICT services in-house.[U1, D7] However, outsourcing greatly limited the possibility of innovation, which hindered the banking sector's potential ability to respond to changing customer demands and trends in a timely manner. By servicing many different financial services providers, the outsourcing companies were able to offer low cost white-labeled financial services.[p151]

Using the next generation of smart phones, telecommunications companies and other new entrants began to provide more and more financial services, with customers using their mobile phones to pay for purchases, manage investments and a range of other financial transactions.[U5, p214, p267] These operations either directly withdrew funds from their bank accounts or were credited to their monthly mobile phone statements. Without the legacy of traditional banks and being much more tuned to the ever-changing demands of their customers, the new entrants were able to react much faster to the changing whim of fickle customers.[p115, p199, p268]

Legend:
- Ux Uncertainties chapter, paragraph number; page 87–95
- Dx Driving forces chapter, paragraph number; page 97–109
- px page number in the Interviews chapter; page 113–269

## 2011–2012

In 2011, IKEA launched a new mortgage scheme, offering customers one of the best interest rates available. The IKEA mortgage included € 20.000+ for the purchase of IKEA products, including free delivery. IKEA made use of the white-labeled products of one of the larger process-driven Indian outsourcing companies, thus rendering obsolete the traditional financial services providers—such as banks. New entrants immediately saw the new opportunities and further increased their financial services by adding low-cost white-labeled financial products.

As financial products became increasingly commoditised, banks had no direct answer to the trend other than to compete on price. Not realising that they needed to proactively meet customers' needs, banks continued to wait for customers to actually tell them what they wanted. They did not realise the enormous advantage of having a wealth of customer information in their databases that could be leveraged into specialised services. However, in order to keep costs low, they increased outsourcing.

By the end of 2012 and following the success of the IKEA mortgage initiative, telephone companies and other new entrants, the number of brands adopting financial services on top of their existing brands, using low-cost white-labeled financial products, p184 greatly increased.• Traditional financial services providers seemed to have no choice but to offer white-labeled products and services to these new entrants in the market if they wanted to maintain profitability. Meanwhile, their own brands, save one or two specialised side brands, lost market shares by the day.

The industry was beginning to feel the benefits of SEPA, which had officially come into effect just two years earlier. Furthermore, in the European elections, the parties in favour of increasing European cooperation received significant support from voters all over Europe. This gave the impression that the public had renewed confidence in One Europe, which further pushed European consolidation.

## 2013–2014

New market entrants pursued banking customers with specific offers. Retiring Boomers, interested in managing and spending, rather than creating wealth, were actively sought by lifestyle financial services providers.• U13 D2.1 Mortgage companies were looking closely at the Millennials, who were well into their professional careers and looking at first mortgages.• U14 D2.2 As marketing campaigns of the new entrants were aimed more at specific target groups, the primary strategy was to appeal to specific lifestyles.• p189 Using new, more flexible risk profiles, built on a wide range of factors and geared to post-industrial working conditions, new service providers were able to play into individual aspirations much more effectively.

By 2014, customers' direct personal contact with banks had decreased as they increasingly turned to virtual and other new service providers, which were better able to anticipate and fulfil their needs. Banks started to reevaluate their position. Observing their new competitors, some banks realised that proactively meeting customer desires was important to regain market share.• p144 p214 Seeing their specialised brands flourish, some of the traditional service providers extended their multilabeling strategy, putting specialised brands in the market for different services. In addition, globalisation, consolidation and resulting saturation of the financial services market meant that specialisation would be the most likely way to increase revenues.• D6 Leveraging the customer information they already had, some banks decided to specialise on their historically core products and services, in order to meet their customers' needs. Other banks, observing that most of their services were already commoditised, concentrated on service excellence and new products, learning from the success of the new entrants.

For example, visualisation technologies were used to create front ends for financial services for simplicity in a world of complicated offerings.• U7 D4 p243 These virtual front ends were created for a range of interfaces. They included the web and personal finance products, new brands and existing personal accounting programs, such as Intuit Quicken and Microsoft Money, which now had the added-value service of anticipatory financial planning, leveraging their own data, rather than simple transaction recording.• D8

Marketing and branding among all market players was intense. As banks found new customers with their multilabel strategy, CRM became increasingly important, but challenged old categories in the Oracle/Siebel system. As there were few, if any, visits to the branches, ICT's role in communication with customers became vital. Systems had to be innovative and flexible to serve the ever-
p177 changing need of customers. ICT ensured the effectiveness and integration of white-label service provision into sophisticated customer front ends. In order to strengthen the customer-bank relationship, these front-end interfaces needed not only to be reliable, understandable and attractive, but anticipatory (enable financial planning) and flexible (geared to individual needs). They needed to
p200 p225 make the complex simple. Competition was stiff and fierce, and customer loyalty could no
p115 longer be depended on.

Elements from both open source software and packages were mixed to create special-
U9 U11 D3 ised services from many different sources. Because of the variety of open source software available, financial services providers adopted a cherry-picking strategy, freely picking and choosing those technologies that best matched their purposes. They were criticised, however, for not contributing to the open source movement.

## 2015–2016

Finally, traditional financial services providers had become more proactive and attentive to customer needs and desires, which helped them to survive in a changing market. The question was, is this "too little too late"?

Many wealthy Boomers had hit retirement. The Boomers unexpectedly chose brands that appealed to them, not incumbent service providers. This meant that Boomers chose many different brands. This showed that traditional concepts of customer segmentation were outdated. In this hyper-commercial world where consumption is key, traditional trust in banks was being replaced by quality of service and value as criteria for choosing a financial services provider.
CRM systems were now expanded to include the process of gathering customer information at every opportunity in order to have
intimate and accurate knowledge available. U6 U10 p220
The information was then used to feed into marketing campaigns.

Internet and web technologies, mobile devices, etc. were developed to reduce complexity for the customer. These technologies U6 U10
allowed financial services providers to offer financial services on nearly every page on the
web as easily as a Google Ad. Visualisation U11
technologies aided financial services providers to make the data visible and transparent to customers while also making the information clear and self-explanatory. These new user interfaces were much simpler and less intimidating, which helped to make the customer's banking experience more pleasant and much less complicated.

## 2017

The global financial economy saw the beginnings of the emergence of large trading blocks around the world. Trade treaties were signed in 2017 among leading economies within three main regions: Europe, Asia and the Americas.

p155 p207 Banking was literally everywhere. Physical branches continued to exist. However, most service centres were found housed within larger organisations that had greater and easier access to customers, such as department stores and supermarkets. financial services, such as loans, were potentially included in the price of any given product, like IKEA mortgages.

Financial products' brands reflected the lifestyle of the customers, similar to other consumer goods, such as clothing, cars and p157 electronic equipment. Along with other products, customers' financial services providers reflected their identity.

The real back-end work for the financial sector was commoditised and done in India, from where companies supplied full-service p250 p255 business processes. The front ends of the financial services were managed in Europe, to service the complicated, individual, fickle, demanding customers. The challenge for ICT in this situation was to become service innovators and to orchestrate a range of increasingly standardised service providers in order to deliver differentiated solutions to demanding individual customers.

Trends moved so quickly that speedy responses to customer demands required a new level of responsiveness from ICT depart- p157 ments. ICT needed to find solutions to flexibly anticipate the fast-moving fashions and p135 individual needs of the customers. ICT's key challenge was in making the complex simple.

The image of Louis Vuitton banking is one of a modern shopping street. But the shopping street, like in westerns, *Lucky Luke* cartoons and film sets, is only a façade to the uniform reality behind it. It is a different icing on the same cake. It is this icing that matters for the customers who go shopping on this street. They want products that are geared to their lifestyle and meet their fickle demands. They go shopping for every service, enjoying the experience and finding

what they need with many different providers.

The role of ICT, as represented by the actors in orange, is to build and maintain the front ends and to keep the channels between front- and back-end systems open and efficient. The bulk of the work is done elsewhere, through Business Process Outsourcing.

# Scenario characteristics

## Cooperation

Companies will compete with each other in offering financial services; many of these companies will be new entrants. Banks will cooperate freely with each other, with larger banks white-labeling ICT providers and business process outsourcing companies that provide fulfillment, while banks provide the actual service.

## Structure of financial services

Banking will literally be everywhere. In every transaction, the possibility of a financial service will be included in the price of the product. For example, IKEA could offer mortgages, white-labeled by large banks, at a reasonable rate, including an allowance for buying IKEA furniture, thereby expanding and locking in its customer base. Specific banking products will also be offered directly by the bank, be it through many specialised brands that banks put in the market.

## Outsourcing

Business process outsourcing (BPO) in the form of white-labeling will be the basis of the structure of financial services in this scenario.

## Global financial health (economy)

Large trading blocks will emerge in the world, dividing into European, Asian and pan-American blocks.

## Demographic perception

Banking services will be geared towards lifestyles, rather than traditional customer segmentation metrics, such as age group or income. This will require a massive reversal and shift of how all financial services will be designed, marketed and consumed.

## Regulations

The regulatory framework of Europe will support European consolidation and encourage transborder competition.

## Globalisation

In this scenario, the response to globalisation will be specialisation, either local- or issue-based. If everything is available everywhere, then financial services providers should specialise, and then market and prove themselves as the best in that particularity.

## Interface technology

Visualisation technologies and interfaces will be paramount in this world. financial services providers will offer a shell on top of a white label, and differentiation will be achieved through branding and service. As there will be many providers, such applications as Google Ads will help the presence and visibility of these providers.

## Physical interface

Physical branches continue to exist, but seldom on their own. They will be part of department stores or could just be a person representing the bank at his/her or your home.

## Web technology

Mashup applications will be created and layered on top of the preexisting software packages. This way, banking can be found on nearly every page on the web, being applied as easily as a Google Ad.

## Back-end technology

Banks will leverage the flexibility of open standards and the structure of software packages, mixing elements from both to create specialised packages from many different sources. While it will not dominate, SOA will play an important role. Best-in-class differentiation will be achieved through benchmarking.

## Open source

A cherry-picking strategy will be dominant. financial services providers will be free to pick and choose those technologies that best match their purposes.

### Europe

As mentioned previously, Europe will be a significant trading block, not only within the borders of the EU, but by extending its trading practices to other trading blocks around the world.

### Customer demand

Customers want their financial services providers to exhibit an instinctive understanding of their needs. These services providers will need to anticipate every whim of the customer, to create packaged services that exactly meet these needs. Fast responses to any new demand, fashion and marketing will be vital as products will experience short life cycles. In order to be closer to the customer and better serve the client's specific demands, many banks will offer specialised services through multilabeling, setting many new labels in the market, next to their main brand, that will be only loosely connected to the banks themselves.

### Role of ICT

The ICT department will ensure the effectiveness and integration of white-label service provision into sophisticated customer front ends. The ICT department's secondary role will be to support the marketing department. Flexibility and thus the ability to respond to the latest fads will be an important consideration in designing the ICT architecture. Every opportunity will be used to gather as much customer information as possible.

### Private banking services

Because there will be many new service providers in the market, there will be many providers for specific services. Customers will be able to pick and choose the best in class and favoured brands to meet their specific demands.

### Retail banking services

Retail banking services will offer a range of multilabeled, specialised products and services that seek to fit to a certain purpose or lifestyle.

### Wholesale financial services

Wholesale financial services will be split into separate functions or areas of capital and advisory.

### SME banking

People will realise that SMEs are a special sector. Boutique financial services providers will offer dedicated services for SME segments.

### Complexity reduction

The combination of speed (i.e., in fashion and marketing), flexibility and integration that is required for this structure will be the main cause of complexity. The main challenge will be in dealing with the complexity of speed.

### CRM

It will be essential to know the market and the customer. Therefore, CRM will be vital to financial institutions. Delivery and branding will be equally important aspects of CRM systems.

### Culture

The culture of experience will dominate. Part of that experience will be the perception that you are getting the best service for the price you are paying for that service. This means that effectiveness will be more important than efficiency.

### Trust

Trust will not be important. As far as trust is concerned, it will play a role and will be mediated by the brand.

## Customer identity

Identities are built by the products that a client buys. In the case of financial products, branded credit cards will serve as an example.

## Loans

Loans will be fully integrated in the price of the product. For example, if you purchase a car or a computer, financing the product will be included in the transaction.

## Bank budgets

Creation of an identity will be vital. Similar to what Nike does now, the total cost of the product will minimally be in the physical product itself; it will mainly be in advertising. A significant part of bank budgets will be set aside to follow fast-moving trends.

Once we understood that it is possible for a gorilla to stare us in the face, beating its chest, without being noticed, we realised that it was time for us to hunt gorillas. What else was staring us in the face without being noticed by us?

Mark Hese

Chapter 4

# Key uncertainties of today's global banking environment





An important distinction of scenario thinking is its emphasis on bringing the hidden into view; on thinking beyond traditional sector developments, and illuminating potential blind spots. It stresses the importance of being prepared for a future in which associated uncertainties can emerge as manageable factors rather than as unexpected obstacles that threaten to derail corporate strategy. Therefore, a first stage in scenario thinking requires participants to identify and assess the key uncertainties in the changing environment that have direct or indirect relevance to the topic at hand.

For the Rabobank-DTN scenario process, more than 20 key uncertainties were identified. This list of topics covered technology, demographics, economic markets, policies and regulations. A select number of these uncertainties are presented in the following pages.

- Outsourcing
- Bank consolidation
- European payments market
- Nontraditional providers
- Mobile banking / e-commerce
- Digitalisation of society
- Visualisation
- Security
- On-demand applications
- Growth of broadband
- Web 2.0
- Impact of aging
- Baby Boomers
- The Millennials
- Immigration

## 1 Outsourcing

Since ICT is often not seen as a core process for financial institutions, outsourcing most, if not the entire, ICT departments of banks has become a growing trend. The main drivers for this development are relatively evident: mounting cost pressures, strong market security and a need to improve stock market performance. This is part of an emerging trend to move away from traditional sourcing relationships and enter partnerships that create value for involved parties.

From the bank's perspective, ICT is not a core competency of a financial institution; making money is the core competency. Therefore, it is logical to outsource the process to a party that can provide the necessary quality of service and enable the organisation to simplify its systems while creating more accountability and stability.

An additional benefit to this is cost reductions. In a report released by the United States Federal Deposit Insurance Corporation (FDIC), noninterest expenses were estimated at 59% of operating revenue for financial institutions. Noninterest expenses include ICT consolidation, inefficient processes, merger-related costs and additional spending on compliance costs. Removing the job of developing and maintaining ICT from the bank's processes would logically result in immediate savings.

## 2 Bank consolidation

There is a general assumption that cross-border consolidation encourages efficient, low-cost banking. Logically, when more efficient banks move across national borders to compete with smaller, less-efficient banks that were formerly protected by the home-nation's legislation, low efficiency will be driven out. Bank consolidation would force all parties to demonstrate performance synergies, almost like a "get with it or get out" strategy. Further, the continued deregulation of barriers to international banking and advances in technology have lowered the costs of supplying cross-border banking services.

Balancing this assumption about low costs are suggested barriers to the continued trend of bank consolidation. They include brand loyalty to local services and the competitive advantages enjoyed by host-nation banks. Countries where host-nation banks hold proprietary knowledge of their own market and possess extensive information about local nonfinancial suppliers and customers are likely to be far less open to integration. Names of foreign banks, especially when attached to well-established entities, are likely to pose difficulties for consumers, who may have trouble recalling the new names. This would call for the newly created bank to invest substantially in public promotion in order to raise brand awareness. Whether the strategy involves retaining the local brand name or promoting a new brand awareness, there will be costs involved in ensuring the success of the newly formed company.

## 3 European payments market

Part of the ongoing transformation of the European payments landscape is the creation of a range of Single Euro Payments Area (SEPA), such as a pan-Europe scheme for e-credit transfers and direct debits. As competition is expected to increase, banks should look to multichannel payment processing. Merchants will look for financial institutions with a flexible infrastructure to offer processing options that provide them with the best possible solutions for each area of business. However, the standardisation of the European payments market is not without problems. Possible barriers to the process include franchise conflict, implementation costs and social challenges.

However, financial institutions may be encouraged by examples such as PayPal, a successful payment service provider. PayPal has no physical branches, drastically reducing overhead costs. It offers electronic payment processing for individuals and retailers alike through several channels: a PayPal account with high-yield interest, direct transfer from a confirmed bank account, credit card payments with major credit card companies and electronic cheques. Furthermore, PayPal offers $1,000 insurance on purchases, bolstering the confidence of its users. Reinforced by a system of user verification and dispute resolution, it has generated a high level of trust among PayPal customers. Its ease of use and global reach have made it a preferred payment provider for a growing number of online retailers, not the least of which is eBay.

## 4 Nontraditional providers

The formerly impenetrable financial market has seen its share of new entrants in the form of software companies, telecommunication companies, online portals, electronic marketplaces and even supermarkets. Creativity, innovation and just plain practicality have driven this change, leading to the emergence of new services. For example, health insurers are assuming the role of banks. As healthcare costs rise, consumers are opting for health savings accounts to alleviate their burden.

Some argue that new entrants to the financial sector can only succeed for durable goods transactions, such as the purchase of home appliances—washing machines, refrigerators—which often involve payment by installment plans: consumers put down a principal amount, and agree to make regular payments over a specified period of time. The appeal of the new entrants cannot be easily dismissed, as they have the ability to track consumer spending habits and detect changes in customer preferences and financial situations, etc., well before their own banks.

In the U.K. alone, more than 11 million people use nontraditional providers (e.g., the local supermarket, post office, etc.) for their savings accounts, credit cards and personal loans. Nontraditional providers have immense potential to differentiate among themselves and to attract customers and assets in the area of financial planning and advice. Recognising that people spend much more time in department stores and supermarkets than they do in their banks, it is easy to detect a looming race for market share, particularly for "emerging wealth" customers.

## 5 Mobile banking / e-commerce

New technologies have enabled faster, easier and more secure access to banking and e-commerce. Asia appears to be a front-runner in the mobile banking race, where it is rapidly gaining popularity for a variety of financial transactions, ranging from micropayments to purchasing shares in the stock market.

In South Korea, almost one million people use their mobile phones to dial into their bank accounts. Kang Chung Wong, CEO of Kookmin, South Korea's biggest bank, attributes m-banking success in South Korea to several conditions:

- Banking services that are secure and easy-to use;

- Support at the government level; and
- A mobile customer base.

Europe has nearly 100% penetration in its mobile phone market, which suggests that mobile banking is a distinct possibility. Branch offices of the banks are not open 24/7. A computer and an Internet connection are not always easily, nor readily, accessible. Mobile phones thus offer more flexibility and connectivity. However, a major drawback may be the type of transaction that currently seems most suitable to mobile banking and e-commerce: simple, straightforward transactions.

## 6 Digitalisation of society

The volume of high-speed Internet connections in the world has grown dramatically. In 2004 alone, the United States saw a 24% increase in Internet subscriptions; the United Kingdom saw an increase of 45%, and France recorded a jump of 59%.

Among other considerations, this suggests an educated consumer. When people can Google for almost any inquiry, the wealth of information at their fingertips and the speed of access means that consumers are able to make much more informed choices. However, in a world of increasing complexity, consumers also risk being stymied by an overabundance of information. To compensate, consumers can seek bundled features in applications, gadgets or services to help simplify their options.

In the end, it is inevitable that the digitalisation of society will have a profound effect on the market. Customer retention may be weakened as the consumer no longer feels brand loyalty. Market winners will be driven to integrate multiple platforms to offer enhanced value, such as multichannel service offerings through physical branches, mobile technology and the Internet.

## 7 Visualisation

According to Wikipedia, data visualisation is the use of "interactive, sensory representations, typically visual, of large amounts of abstract data to reinforce cognition, hypothesis building and reasoning."

Interest in applying visualisation concepts to the banking environment has been fueled by the rapid development of graphical processing units (GPUs) and game consoles, which has established the computational layer for large complex data representations. Looking at financial information is probably not the most engaging activity for the average person. It is equally as unlikely that the average person will glean a clear understanding of complex financial information from charts or standard bar graphs.

With the acceptance of better visualisation in presenting financial data, particularly complex sets of data, financial institutions will enable novel and insightful interpretations by a larger audience.

## 8 Security

Security is perhaps a bank's greatest risk in terms of brand damage. Should it become known that a bank's firewall has been breached, it is highly unlikely—or it will be with great difficulty and cost—that the bank can recover from the attack. Phishing and spoofing in order to access a financial institution's confidential customer account information are not uncommon incidents. Despite bank vigilance, raising the awareness of such activities, and encouraging customers to be actively involved in discouraging such activities, many people continue to fall prey to phishing and spoofing attacks.

Despite the significance of such security risk, ICT is considered to be a noncore function of a financial institution. Credit Suisse, for example, outsourced its security to Ubizen to monitor the bank's intrusion detection system. It considered the level of complexity required for monitoring and administering the ICT environment to be very knowledge-specific and specialised, and not readily available within the bank.

Security is, therefore, a major uncertainty. The entertainment industry, which often conveys serious issues in a less-than-serious manner, sent a sobering message in the latest installment of the *Die Hard* movie series, "Live Free or Die Hard." It tells the story of a group of techno-terrorists who attempt to bring down a country by shutting down its transportation system, financial infrastructure and utilities grid. The terrorists hack into the computer system of the New York Stock Exchange, changing stock prices to show a severe drop across the board, and incite mass panic. While the movie is fictional, the hacking activities are close to reality, sending a clear signal about ICT security issues of consequence to financial institutions. As *Star Trek* communicators have shown with regard to mobile phones, the stuff of yesterday's fiction may be the reality of tomorrow.

## 9 On-demand applications

On-demand applications are task-oriented business solutions delivered in a timely manner. These applications allow the user to "cherry-pick" application features, which have been broken down into individual components and put together into a tailored application package for the user.

Two primary drivers steered the emergence of on-demand applications:

- Escalating frustration with the hassles and costs of implementing complex applications with features that have little to no use for the user; and
- The emergence of technologies that permit traditional packaged applications to be exchanged for Internet-based services.

Although the marketing of on-demand applications has been picked up by companies, such as Oracle/Siebel with its CRM On-Demand service, the applications are seen to present significant drawbacks. First, companies within the same industry may not see a clear differentiation among the application packages; and, indeed, there may not be much difference. Second, it is possible that on-demand applications are serviceable for 80% of standard processes, but the remaining 20%, which represent the companies' key differentiators in the market, must be undertaken by traditional vendors with specific industry expertise.

## 10 Growth of broadband

According to the Ipsos News Center's annual "The Face of the Web" report, around 77% of the global online population was using broadband connections, versus 21% for dial-up technology, by the end of 2006. In the United States, the average length of time spent online by an individual is around 14 hours per week, which is high and is roughly equal to the amount of time spent watching television. Online consumers spent an average of $11.7 billion between

January to November 2006. Although broadband Internet access appears to be peaking and markets are reaching saturation, it is widely believed that wireless connectivity will be the next phase of global Internet usage.

The rapid penetration of broadband can be seen in the examples of South Korea and Hong Kong, which already offer 1 Gbps broadband services. By the time Hong Kong rolled out its service in April 2005 for a monthly fee of $215, 800,000 out of 2.2 million households had already subscribed for the service, demonstrating how consumers value speed of broadband services over packaged bundles offered by Internet service providers.

More countries are expected to have high-speed, high-availability broadband services. While this provides encouragement for developing and launching new technologies, there is some need for caution. The state of the underlying infrastructure may not be sufficiently developed. Voice-over-IP initially failed because the underlying infrastructure was unable to deliver the desired results. Thus, the failure of new technologies should not be discounted; nor should their success be seen as a given based on the availability of high-speed services. Instead, the maturation of the underlying infrastructure will be a key factor in the successful and widespread adoption of new technologies.

## 11 Web 2.0

Although Web 2.0 is a concept that eludes easy definitions, it can generally be seen as the confluence of bottom-up, web-enabled technologies and organisational processes that represent a new social, organisational and technological paradigm. This suggests, among other things, that the next evolutionary phase of the Internet will be driven by the contrasting dynamics created by bottom-up versus top-down processes.

The application layer for Web 2.0 is provided by open source software, as shown in the open API wave pioneered by such companies as Google, Craigslist.com and Amazon. Information content has also been reorganised. Despite the initial skepticism, the continued popularity of Wikis and Wikipedia, where users can generate, edit and update their own content, shows that the model works.

The Web 2.0 revolution could kick off a new Internet boom-bust cycle. At the very least, it presents a completely new and compelling Internet paradigm.

## 12 Impact of aging

Over the last 160 years, the average human life expectancy has consistently increased by three months per year in developed countries. The "graying" populations of developed countries are expected to have major implications for the global market. Italy alone expects the number of its citizens between the ages of 20 to 64 to decrease by 37% between 2000 to 2050, while the number of people aged 65 and above is expected to increase by 72% in the same period of time.

The "graying" phenomenon is not limited to developed nations. It is expected to affect China as well. Almost a quarter of China's population is expected to be over 65 years of age by 2030, with the proportion stabilising at approximately 21% to 22% by 2040. In the United Kingdom and in most European countries, this figure will stabilise at around 14% to 18%. Although the changing demographics could be taken as a signal of difficult times ahead, the future is subject to other variables and unknowns that could mitigate or further deepen a bleak outlook. If the dependency ratios—i.e., the proportion of people over 65 years of age relative to the proportion aged 15 to 65,—remain low, the economy could cope with a graying population. However, if the ratio increases, the risk of a problematic future increases. Will the trend stop growth? The next five to 10 years could bring a shift from net inflow of cash to net outflow, but this is not inevitable. At the very least, however, the anticipation of a more difficult future will psychologically drive different behaviour.

## 13 Baby Boomers

In the United States alone, there are 77 million people who belong to the Baby Boomer generational group. This generation has long been a target of interest for the financial sector. Expected to enter retirement over the next 10 years, Baby Boomers represent an "emerging wealth" market with individual assets of $50,000–$500,000 each.

With retirement on the horizon, the Baby Boomers are expected to be planning their financial security. However, contrary to logical expectations, a report by Celent, published in June 2005, suggests that financial institutions rank last in overall impact on the financial planning of this group. The report found that Baby Boomers prefer to rely on their own research as the primary source of financial information. This raises the risk of poor-quality information leading to poor financial choices that could adversely affect retirement savings.

By 2025, one in five Europeans will be above 65 years of age. It is expected that the absolute level of savings will dramatically decrease across most of Europe as the population of working people in Europe drops by 20.8 million over the next 25 years. This, in turn, implies that people will wish to change retirement plans, finding a need to work longer, retire later and insure against sickness, aging and their greatest insecurity: the unpredictable costs of catastrophic illness and care.

## 14 The Millennials

The Millennials comprise a demographic group of more than 60 million in the United States alone. Born approximately between 1980 and 2000, this group has many names—Generation Y, Echo Boomers and Nintendo Generation, to name a few. Because of its size, this group is expected to have economic and social impacts like the Baby Boomers.

As consumers, the Millennials are the biggest youth spenders in history. With a purchasing power of over $200 billion, Millennials not only spend money, but they also influence the purchasing decisions of their peers and their parents. Their attitude towards work is to operate smartly, compensating by using many technologies to get the job done efficiently, enabling them to maintain a work-life balance. They may lack the skills and experience of the many retirees they are now replacing and will continue to replace, but they are expected to depend on technology to fill this gap.

Their effect on the financial sector will be considerable. Banks will recruit employees from their ranks and seek to sign them on as customers. Because Millennials are recognised to be experienced consumers who seek convenience and accessibility, banks will need to establish a strategy for attracting and retaining Millennials as clients who will require a departure from previous ways of doing business.

## 15 Immigration

Immigration is often offered as a solution to the problem of aging populations in the developed world. While the position remains arguable, it remains an important consideration in debates about immigration policy. However, if immigration is the solution to a "graying" Europe, the region could find itself in difficulty. Germany, the European Union's largest economy, shows a decline in the net inflow of newcomers. It recorded an overall net immigration figure of only 75,000 in 2004. This is a significant drop from 400,000 10 years ago, and an average of 200,000 between 2000 to 2003. Germany's example and the trend towards tighter immigration policies suggest that immigration is on a decline in Europe as a whole.

Despite concerns that immigration will lead to fewer jobs for a country's nationals, the benefits of immigration are well recognised in countries with an immigration culture. Immigration has the potential to increase economic growth and decrease unemployment. Newcomers boost consumption and drive economic demand, benefiting sectors from housing to retail, and helping industries such as construction, real estate, etc. While immigration increases the number of job seekers in the labour market, it has also been shown that newcomers often take jobs that are passed up by others who are unwilling; and that the economic benefits they bring drive economic demand, which results in the creation of new jobs. Further, about 60% of immigrants are between the ages of 18 to 40, placing them far from retirement age. Because of their relative youth, they are among the healthier populace, bringing less demand on the healthcare system.

Immigration has given banks a new opportunity for business: remittances, which are disposable income sent home, usually to developing nations. In 2004, the official remittance cash flow was in the area of $167 billion; in the US, the Hispanic community alone accounted for $32 billion of that figure. More and more banks are finding ways to help transfer this money at lower costs, and to establish credit and teach about small investments. However, a significant obstacle in the trend is security concerns. In today's global climate, concerns about terrorist financing and money laundering have imposed impediments to private financial flows.

Chapter 5

# Driving forces: Shaping the future

The uncertainties workshop provided an opportunity to explore the changing landscape for ICT in banking; and to define the challenges that could emerge in the future. As the next step, the core team examined the engines of change that are driving these uncertainties. Although these forces may not always be open to influence, any strategic planning, if it is to be sound and robust, should be cognizant of them and prepared. The following driving forces were identified by the team:

- Global financial crisis
- Demographics
- Web 2.0
- Data visualisation
- Regulations and compliance
- Globalisation
- Outsourcing
- Flat-layered computing
- Open banking
- Mashups

## 1 Global financial crisis

Despite clear signals, financial crises often take most people by surprise when they occur. Once possible to limit to a country or specific region, in today's globalised environment—for example, integration is particularly tight where capital markets are concerned—financial contagion can quickly spread across continents, much like a line of falling dominoes. Ignoring signs of a pending financial crisis can be disastrous as financial volatility brings about massive economic breakdown with a range of consequences, such as general insecurity, unemployment, loss of income, assault on working conditions, increased social tensions, population shifts, outbreak of conflict, popular dissent, etc.

It is generally understood that economies go through cycles: "what goes up must come down." In the 1920s, Russian economist Nikolai Kondratieff theorized that the global economy goes through a 70-year cycle. This cycle has become known as the Kondratieff Wave.

The Kondratieff Wave has four distinct phases, or "seasons." "Spring" is the period after a depression when the economy is relatively debt-free and people have replenished savings. "Summer" is characterized by sharply rising prices and interest rates; a sharp, but brief, recession follows the summer peak. "Autumn" sees a bullish market, following a peak in interest rates and commodity prices. Finally, as the cycle enters "winter," the market enters a bearish run, and prices and interest rates drop sharply, entering a period of depression.

Because the cycle generally lasts for 70 years, each phase of the cycle is a once-in-a-lifetime event. This implies that the next generation is unable to learn the lessons from its predecessors, and is doomed to go through the cycle, unable to avoid the "winter." If we stipulate that our current cycle began in 1949, and the Kondratieff Wave model holds true, then the global economy is due for a shake-up.

Based upon research and observation, as well as interviews with experts, there are four possible triggers for a global financial crisis:

- Rising U.S. national debt and the fall of the dollar;
- Peak oil;
- Increasing climate volatility due to climate change; and
- A global flu pandemic.

### 1.1 Rising U.S. national debt and the fall of the dollar

Lower interest rates typically weaken a currency by cutting into investor returns on the assets that are denominated in the currency. At the time of the Rabobank scenario process, the U.S. national debt was just under $9.0 trillion, with an average daily debt increment of $3.48 billion (March 2006). Today, the U.S. national debt is just above $9.1 trillion, with an average daily debt increment of $1.51 billion. Close to 50% of the US public debt is held by foreign governments and banks, primarily in Asia. In March 2006, Japan was the largest holder of Treasury bonds with $668 billion; and China held $263 billion in securities. By September 2007, Japan was still the largest holder of US securities at $582.2 billion, but China has closed the gap with holdings of $396.7 billion.

The dollar has been dropping steadily since 2000. This is driving a declining interest of foreign investors to continue investing in dollar denominated instruments. However, for now, a significant amount of U.S. public debt is still being held in the hands of foreigners. At the very least, this situation has the potential to compromise future U.S. foreign trade dealings.

The weakening dollar has stimulated calls for shifting the petrodollar to the petroeuro. Should this happen, countries would no longer need to retain U.S. dollars as reserve currency. If countries decrease their U.S. dollar reserve currency, dropping the demand for U.S. dollars, the value of the U.S. dollar will fall even further. Fewer people would then want to purchase U.S. debt, which means that the interest rate on U.S. debt would increase significantly. The United States would find itself in a quagmire from which it would be extremely difficult to emerge.

A lack of sound financial education can partly be blamed for the current situation the United States finds itself in. People spend recklessly on credit, with little to no savings, and with no clear strategy for repayment. Their situation is not helped by the prohibitive costs of higher education and the rising costs of healthcare.

## 1.2 Peak oil

Given that oil is a non-renewable resource, it is natural to assume that total oil production will increase and eventually decline. M. King Hubbard predicted this curve in 1957, also known as Hubbard's curve. While the supply of oil is declining, the global demand for oil is increasing. The global population grows ever larger, and China and Asia grows ever hungrier for resources—world-wide oil demand will at some point actually exceed supply.

There are differing opinions as to when oil production will "peak", and the estimates vary from 2000–2015; but the broad consensus is that it will steadily "decline", raising oil prices. Oil prices are expected to average $85 per barrel in 2008. A future of $100 per barrel is imminent.

## 1.3 Climate change

Warmer temperatures and rising sea levels are some of the seemingly innocuous trends. But, in truth, these indications of global warming are causing the more violent natural disasters that we have witnessed in the last ten years. For example, Hurricane Katrina resulted in $300 billion in damages, and dislocated about 500,000 people, giving rise to a new term, "the climate refugee."

What are the implications of climate change for the financial sector? Insurance companies alone will be crippled, unable to survive another catastrophe of the same scale as Hurricane Katrina. With rising sea levels, coastal areas are especially vulnerable. It is expected that people living in coastal areas will need to be evacuated and relocated to higher ground. The associated costs of such events are astronomical.

## 1.4 Global pandemic

The spectrum of estimates for the next flu pandemic range from optimistic (i.e., 700,000 deaths globally) to severe (i.e., 142 million deaths globally). The increased mobility of people (i.e., international air travel) will aid the rapid spread of the virus. The virus could spread throughout a small country in a matter of weeks; across all continents in a matter of months.

High numbers of illness, inadequate medical supplies and personnel, and the large number of deaths globally will cause significant worker absenteeism. In other words, a global flu pandemic will result in massive social and economic disruptions. Although these disruptions will be temporary, in a world of interrelationships and interdependencies, these disruptions in supply of essential services, such as power, transportation and communication, would be nothing short of disastrous. Futhermore, recovery would be hampered by fear. The tourism industry is likely to see a dramatic drop in traffic. There will also likely be a drop in import-export activities, partially owing to trade and transportation restrictions.

Any of these four possible events would be enough to cause a major disruption of the world economy, although perhaps not an economic breakdown. However, given the fragility of the dollar, rising oil prices, volatile climate change and the possibility of an influenza pandemic, there is a realistic possibility that these events could occur in conjunction, and the notion of a global economic crisis cannot be dismissed. The fear of a global financial crisis is driving the financial sector towards greater international cooperation to find solutions and remedial actions for a possible future of large shake-ups, bank defaults, economic deceleration and a global move towards a recession and reverse globalisation.

## 2 Demographics

The global birthrate is declining. Some experts predict that the world population will peak in 2050 at 8.9 billion and then decline. It is generally acknowledged that the populations of developed nations are graying rapidly, and that the actual birth rate is below the 2.1 replacement rate. This graying phenomenon is not limited to developed nations alone. China's population is also graying rapidly. By 2040, 400 million people in China will be over 60 years of age. The changing demographics have serious implications for the financial environment.

### 2.1 Baby Boomers

As Baby Boomers age and enter retirement, they will continue to spend money. As their health worsens, sufficient funds for medical care will become priority. For financial institutions, Baby Boomers could trigger a wave of growth in financial planning as they rush to save for retirement. The U.S. financial sector expects this "emerging wealth" group to inherit $1 trillion over the next 15 years.

In anticipation of Boomer retirement, governments expect to see huge increases in pension and healthcare costs, undercutting economic growth. Government pension plans, which would have only worked under a steady growth-rate scenario, are unable to cover all of the Boomer generation's needs and still meet the needs of future generations. However, Boomers themselves have given rise to a new trend. Instead of entering full retirement, many Boomers plan to continue to work or to shift between work and leisure cycles, thereby affording them increased earnings, savings and compounding years. In this way, they will not be expected to begin using their retirement savings as a primary source of income until much later than is expected. While this means that there will be more people in the job market, it also means a much lower financial burden on younger generations.

### 2.2 The Millennials

In the United States, the Millennials drive the retail economy. With purchasing power of almost $200 billion per year, this group is consumer friendly, and thus dominates the U.S. economy and drives American product innovation. In contrast, the Millennials do not receive much attention in Europe, the focus being predominantly on Baby Boomers. However, this focus is slowly shifting.

The Millennials are innately comfortable and skilled in today's ICT environment. Having grown up with the Internet, they are aware of hacking, phishing and spoofing activities. They know how easy it is to run a con operation over the Internet. Their experiences and their knowledge make them cynical regarding big-brand advertising. The Millennials are a hard sell. They will not remain loyal to a brand they cannot connect with or one that does not resonate with them. Brands will find themselves coming under hard and constant scrutiny by these young consumers.

The Millennials are also probably one of the most pampered generations ever known. They have come to expect a certain quality of life. This represents a significant opportunity for financial institutions. Millennials will require money to finance and maintain that high quality of life. Sound and early financial planning will be in high demand, but only if Millennials can connect the necessity of financial planning with the values and needs they hold dear.

### 2.3 Immigration

The population growth in most developed countries has fallen below the replacement rate of 2.1 children per woman. Immigration is a possible solution to this dilemma. Immigration is helping developed countries meet their need for skilled workers. This trend will accelerate as the workforce in the West ages and education levels continue to rise in emerging economies. Another benefit of immigration is that the majority of immigrants are fairly young, usually between 18 to 40 years old. Therefore, they are expected to put less strain on the pension and the healthcare system.

Immigrants bring energy, optimism and, often, financial wealth to their new homes. They represent an opportunity for financial services institutions in terms of new business, both for standard savings services and for mortgage loans, as immigrants are most likely in the market to invest in property. Furthermore, because native Europeans tend to marry late and have few or no children, Europe's demographic profile is expected to shift to a majority immigrant population.

The aging of Baby Boomers, the entrance of the Millennials into the workforce and immigrantion flows are changing the demographic landscape of Western nations. Financial service institutions will need to rediscover who their customers are and how to best provide them with financial products and services. A one-for-all strategy will no longer be sufficient to satisfy an increasingly diverse clientele.

## 3 Web 2.0

A basic description offered by O'Reilly media's CEO Tim O'Reilly is noteworthy for examining Web 2.0 as a driving force. Web 2.0 has no hard boundary, but rather a gravitational core. Surrounding this gravitational core is a set of principles and practices that form the "solar system" of websites that demonstrate some or all of those principles.

Web 2.0 acknowledges the power of the "long tail," which is composed of the collective power of the small sites that make up the bulk of the web's content. Companies that embrace the Web 2.0 concept understand the long tail and are able to reach a much wider customer base. Web 2.0 companies understand the power of knowledge. Data management is a core competency of Web 2.0 companies. Successful Web 2.0 companies create their own data and certain classes of data—location, identity, calendaring of public events, product identifier, namespaces, etc. These companies then become the single source for the data. Another possibility for a company to succeed in a Web 2.0 environment is to be the first to reach critical mass via user aggregation and turn aggregated data into a system service.

Web 2.0 companies leverage their users, enabling their users to add value, so that the service or product gets better the more people use it. BitTorrent, a peer-to-peer file-sharing communications protocol, is an example of a Web 2.0 trend. Each person who logs on to the network becomes another server to share the data. Network effects from user contributions are the key to market dominance in the Web 2.0 era.

Unlike the model of proprietary software, Web 2.0 service software is designed for "hackability" and "remixability." The barriers to reuse are low, which promotes innovation and creativity. Mashups, which will be discussed in a later section, are a perfect example of the Web 2.0 solar system.

Web 2.0 companies deliver software as a service, not as a product. If software is delivered as a service, the software will cease to perform unless it is maintained on a daily basis. Continuous improvement is one of the key success factors of a Web 2.0 company, the core competency being real-time monitoring of user behaviour to see exactly which new features are used and how they are used. Web 2.0 users are treated as co-developers.

The appeal of Web 2.0 lies in the ease with which it allows people to actively participate in online activities and engage in social networking. Because Web 2.0 applications leverage collective intelligence for continuous improvement, financial institutions can take full advantage of this model to improve customer service and user experience, increase the flexibility of customer service, and minimize those extraneous costs that are implicit in the current organisational structure.

## 4 Data visualisation

Data visualisation technology provides an intuitive graphical interface, based on interactive visual metaphors, for exploring data. It can be a powerful tool for gaining useful insights into massive amounts of data. Advances in computing power, collection techniques and data mining technology are generating vast quantities of data. In particular, clusters and their associated datasets are so large (in the order of 1 terabyte/hour) that it is nearly impossible to start looking for interesting data. Visualisation offers a tool through which one can more effectively and efficiently extract pertinent information or conduct more focused information searches. Raw data, while essential, may not be particularly useful. In order to extract useful information from raw data, one needs to see it through visualisation. In a business context, data visualisation can enable business users to glean useful information from their business data for faster and more informed decision making.

The benefits of data visualisation are manifold. It can address any real-world data and message. Pure tables of numbers can be difficult to interpret to the untrained eye. Graphs allow readers to visualize complex datasets in a simpler, more concise manner. Data visualisation also offers a comprehensive set of graphical displays, which enables users to see the data from several different perspectives. Trends within a database can be detected and explored.

As a driving force for the financial sector, data visualisation shows the potential for banks to internally manage their organisations more effectively, as well as bring coherency to the vast array of financial information at their disposal.

## 5 Regulations and compliance

Ever since the Enron and WorldCom scandals, governments and organisations have been working towards greater transparency. In Europe, these developments are coupled with the changing EU regulatory landscape. Initiatives such as Basel II, the Lisbon Agenda, SEPA and Sarbanes-Oxley mean that financial services institutions are experiencing rising, and potentially prohibitive, costs of implementation and compliance.

## 5.1 Basel II

The Basel II is an international initiative that requires financial services institutions to have a more risk-sensitive framework for the assessment of regulatory capital. It was designed to improve transparency in financial institutions by making it a requirement to disclose substantially more information to stakeholders than is the current practice.

Compliance costs were estimated to be between €50 million (for smaller banks with assets of less than US $100 billion) to €115 million (for larger banks). The final count is unknown, but it is generally accepted that the actual compliance costs far exceeded expectations.

## 5.2 The Lisbon Agenda

The Lisbon Agenda is a set of strategies for making the EU the most dynamic and competitive knowledge-based economy in the world by 2010. It set targets to achieve an average rate of 3% overall economic growth for the EU-25, and to create 20 million jobs by 2010. In order to accomplish these targets, the Lisbon Agenda lays out a set of goals that covers such areas as employment, innovation, enterprise, liberalisation and environment:

- Employment: to raise the employment rate to 70% of the population;
- Innovation: to provide more Internet access and spend more on research and development;
- Enterprise: to give more support to small and medium-sized enterprises (SMEs) and reduce regulation;
- Liberalisation: to increase competition in telecom, gas and electricity markets; and
- Environment: to reduce greenhouse gas emissions.

Underlying the Lisbon Agenda is an understanding that the role of ICT is crucial for its success. The Lisbon Agenda states explicitly that ICT plays a critical role in ensuring trust and strengthening transparency by making information more accessible to the public. As such, the EU will need to increase the security level of its ICT systems at the very least.

## 5.3 SEPA

European banks are focused on the creation of a Single Euro Payments Area (SEPA) as one way of addressing the necessary gaps in the European payments arena. The fees charged by existing payments systems cover only 10–15% of the actual cost of running these systems. The primary reason for this significant gap is the way payments are processed. Payments processing occurs in back offices, where major costs are incurred, and is fragmented across the different business lines of a bank.

SEPA is expected to increase competition through the reduction of the number of banking relationships at the local level. Banks are forced to develop new payment strategies and services to attract and retain customers, and increase revenues to make up for lost transaction fees.

SEPA is incurring a lot of costs for the financial sector. Like Basel II, development and implementation costs for SEPA are exorbitant, allocated to building a new and robust payments-related infrastructure. Although SEPA is targeted to go into effect in 2010, the high costs are acting as a barrier to greater involvement by financial services institutions.

SEPA is only one of the factors driving changes in the payments industry, but it acts as an accelerator for preparations to meet a very different business environment in the future. Ongoing customisation of the payments industry, changing business models (i.e., customer-centricity) and changing corporate customer needs and behaviours are other factors affecting the financial sector. Compliance with SEPA acts as an accelerator and forces banks to carefully consider how their payments infrastructure must evolve to accommodate a highly competitive and commoditised business environment—a vastly different arena than in the past when banks enjoyed a highly lucrative and safe revenue stream.

### 5.4 Sarbanes-Oxley

Sarbanes-Oxley, or SOx for short, is U.S. legislation that was passed in 2002 in response to a string of corporate governance and accounting scandals, most notably Enron and WorldCom. It set up an industry watchdog, called the Public Company Accounting Oversight Board, or PCAOB, as part of an effort to strengthen corporate governance and restore investor confidence.

Technically, SOx is only applicable to public companies; however, private companies also find themselves affected. Costs of compliance, audit and certification are high, hitting SMEs particularly hard. Cost aside, SOx reforms have made it increasingly difficult for banks to prepare for the turn in the credit cycle. In the past, banks increase reserves during good times to prepare for future loan defaults during poor times. Under SOx, banks are forced to cut these reserves, which help to absorb the impact of the inevitable deterioration of credit quality at the end of the credit cycle.

The added cost burden of regulations and compliance-related challenges are driving the banking sector towards industry consolidation, increased software standardisation with vendors that specialise in handling compliance systems, heightened security measures and outsourcing.

## 6 Globalisation

Globalisation is often perceived as the spread of influence from West to East, North to South. However, the global environment has changed such that globalisation now implies the reversal of these dynamics, so that the influence is spreading from East to West, South to North.

Emerging markets play an important role in the changing dynamics of globalisation. Over the next 50 years, developed nations will have powerful new economic partners or rivals in developing countries, such as India, China and Brazil. Emerging market companies have several factors working in their favour. They have:

- Advantage of wide-open world economy;
- Easy access to Western knowledge and talent;
- Vast supply of money from global capital markets;
- Low-cost skilled domestic labour; and
- Highly adaptive skills honed by surviving regular financial crises and domestic political chaos.

The most significant challenge to Western companies exists not within their own borders, but within the borders of developing nations themselves. These countries have the distinct advantage of being able to supply goods and services that are simply cheaper, more user-friendly and more effectively distributed. In addition, existing close cultural ties in growing regional markets enhance this advantage.

C.K. Prahalad, renowned strategist and author of *The Fortune at the Bottom of the Pyramid*, is an ardent advocate of the belief that the poor should not be considered a burden to society, but rather "resilient and creative entrepreneurs and value-conscious consumers." There are 4 to 5 billion potential consumers at the bottom of the pyramid (BOP). Seen in this light, BOP consumers represent a huge potential for driving innovations in technology, products and services, as well as new business models that could be the catalyst for the next global economic boom.

### 6.1 Glocalisation

A combination drawn from "globalisation" and "localisation," glocalisation is defined by Wikipedia as the "creation or distribution of products and services intended for a global or transregional market, but customised to suit local laws or culture." Although the term is new, the phenomenon is not. McDonald's, which has been around since 1940, is an example of a glocalised company. It has a global presence with standard menu items, but local branches within each country add local specialities to the menu; such as the McKroket in the Netherlands or the Bulgogi Burger in South Korea.

The term "glocalisation" represents a new dynamic management model that is driven by the globalisation of products, processes and people, and the reconciliation of regional, local and global management. In Europe, where there is a wide mix of cultures, histories, trends and economies, this management model will prove useful.

Globalisation will drive the financial services industry towards the glocalisation of products and services to suit its customer base and their preferences, culture, ethnicity and background. Globalisation will also offer opportunities to create more services and investments, such as microfinancing, for BOP customers. The consolidation of the financial sector will be an effect of globalisation, and increased global competition will force each individual organisation to rethink its brand and service offerings in order to differentiate itself from competitors.

## 7 Outsourcing

Cost pressures, strong market scrutiny and the need to improve stock market performance continue to drive the trend for outsourcing noncore business components. Companies outsource functions that are not considered a core business function in an effort to minimize unnecessary costs and to focus on their core competencies. Since ICT is often seen as a noncore function, it is therefore one of the primary functions outsourced to third-party companies.

The current trend in ICT outsourcing is to move away from long-term contracts towards those that are well-defined and of limited scope. Five-year contracts are now considered too long-term, given that both the world and technology have a tendency to change rapidly. These changes lower costs, but companies remain trapped in outdated contracts. Therefore, the move now is towards component or modular services. For example, when a financial company needs to get a sophisticated product to market quickly, the increasing complexity calls for a provider of specialised or modular services to step in specifically for that single product.

Outsourcing the ICT department may sound like a solution. However, banks must continue to maintain a small ICT department within the organisation. This remaining unit would necessarily be coached to interact successfully with third-party suppliers. Furthermore, the much-smaller ICT department must be better at different tasks than those typically undertaken by a full department. For example, the new ICT department would need to develop a competency to work in partnership with a supplier and excel at understanding the business in order to become a business partner, rather than just a small functionality.

Outsourcing may be seen as an outgrowth of the globalisation process. The first generation of outsourcing involved product manufacturing in developing countries such as China, because labour and production costs were substantially lower than in domestic manufacturing. Next came outsourcing services, such as ICT services. ICT outsourcing is expected to mature within the next few years. The third generation of outsourcing will then proceed naturally to process outsourcing, such as for mortgage or payments processes. Going forward, we may expect banks to explore other avenues for transferring work offshore.

Some problems and challenges have been raised regarding current perceptions and expectations for outsourcing. Among them are that the outsourced party should not be seen as problem solvers, and that companies seeking to outsource processes should not do so with the mindset of passing on the problem to someone else. The required condition for process outsourcing is that the process does not have preexisting problems. Second, within the next decade, the costs of ICT services in India, the current favourite for outsourcing, will be approximately the same level as it is now in the West. Third, mature processes are easy to outsource, but at some point, innovation resulting from changing technologies inevitably interrupts the process.

The experience of the banking sector with outsourcing shows that outsourcing is not a cure-all for problems in existing products and services. The banking sector is also beginning to realise that the cost benefits derived from outsourcing to low-cost third parties will not last indefinitely.

## 8 Flat-layered computing

Flat-layered computing is driven by the confluence of several trends:

- Massively parallel redundant clusters;
- Databases;
- Search technologies; and
- Structured record keeping.

### 8.1 Massively parallel redundant clusters

During the 1980s, a new paradigm in computing emerged under the tutelage of Danny Hillis. With a background in biology and mathematics, Hillis wanted to build computers that could use lessons learnt from biology, not from telecommunications; that is, systems that were massively parallel, redundant and able to repair themselves. Hillis brought his ideas to fruition in the company/research project Thinking Machines. Thinking Machines built the Connection machine, which in its first iteration had custom processors. Toward the end of the project, the company shifted its approach to using inexpensive hardware, which allowed for large-scale clusters to be built. This proved to be a breakthrough in creating large computing systems.

## 8.2 Databases

Large-scale systems in the 1970s and 1980s have been designed around three specific constraints:

- Limited storage space (primary storage);
- Limited addressable problem space (memory); and
- Limited computing power (and available in small blocks).

In order to develop within the above constraints, databases formed the ideal solution. Databases, with their structured record-keeping systems, do much of the processing at the point of data capture. By intelligently designing data structures, programmers can create much faster, smaller, more elegant and hard-to-maintain systems. Because processes are combined with data, it is almost impossible to adapt and grow these systems without revisiting the original designs. This, coupled with unexpected interactions between different sets of data in the databases, is one of the key constraints of developing and maintaining legacy systems.

However, none of the above three constraints still apply. Storage space is plentiful and cheap, and can be redundantly kept spinning. Also, 64-bit processors create vast addressable problem spaces, and computing power in clusters is cheap and plentiful. Therefore, it is possible to have dramatically different design approaches to large-scale systems.

## 8.3 Search technologies

One of the unexpected developments of the last 16 years of the public Internet is the rapid and robust development of search technologies. Search technologies allow powerful user interaction with unstructured data. Search technology today can deliver the same query facilities that databases used to deliver in the past.

## 8.4 Structured record keeping

Databases essentially are structured record-keeping systems, such as the file system. It is possible to use the file system, which is much more scalable, reliable and robust, to store data in a structured fashion. This, in combination with search technologies, can effectively copy the functionality of databases without the overhead to create powerful, reliable, redundant and seamlessly scalable systems.

## 8.5 Flat-layered computing: design approach

Brewster Kahle who worked at and then left Thinking Machines, started the search engine, Alexa Internet, which was later bought by Amazon. The design philosophy was refined and promoted at Kahle's next initiative, the Internet Archive. A free, robust operating system, Linux, provided the operating system layer. This led to the inspiration for Google's computing approach. Today, Google—with, perhaps, the exceptions of NSA, NASA and Schlumberger—has the largest computing clusters in the world. With 100,000+ machines, Google could not grow or function as a business without an inexpensive approach to computing. In the absence of an existing term, we have provisionally called this "flat-layered computing."

Hypothetically, it is possible to design the technical systems of a bank at a fraction of the cost and maintainability. At the very least, flat-layered computing is a significant driving force for the banking sector because new entrants and innovation will continuously enter the market. The rate of these new market entrants and the rapid introduction of innovation implies that banks will find it difficult to keep up with faster, smaller and more innovative players.

## 9 Open banking

In a traditional banking structure, in its broadest definition, the bank acts as a money depository for its clients. Under this model, clients entrust the bank to keep their money safe, or to offer sound financial planning advice. The bank thus acts as an intermediary between the clients and potential investment opportunities, but neither side comes into contact with the other. This top-down approach also means that clients often do not know who is on the other side of the table, or how their money is being used.

The advent of Web 2.0 has introduced new tools that allow for collaboration, not only on a local scale, but also globally. In this new environment, the bank acts as an intermediary partner, not unlike how eBay is an intermediary partner between auction buyers and sellers. In this instance, banks can match the millions of people needing small loans with people who have the cash to lend.

This has huge implications for the future roles of ICT and the ICT department in banks. Bank ICT departments will shift their role to create a platform where money does not actually go to the bank. The money will go directly from people who need to spend it and want to invest it to people who need it. Like eBay, the bank acts as a credit-rating provider or advisor, participating either directly or indirectly in transactions, effectively creating an efficient bottom-up system. The bank will generate revenue by building and creating this platform and convincing people to buy into it, as not everyone is automatically accepted on the platform.

Matching people who need small loans with others who have the extra cash to lend is not a novel idea. Peer-to-peer banking has cropped up from California to the United Kingdom. Under the open banking structure of peer-to-peer banks, borrowers need to undergo mandatory identity and credit checks. They may also post bids specifying how much they wish to borrow as well as the highest interest rate they are willing to pay. In turn, lenders submit a bid for the lowest rate they will accept for a given credit profile as well as the period for the loan. These open banks function as managers for the repayment of loans and are in charge of hiring debt collectors should a borrower default. The banks earn money by charging borrowers a small percentage of the amount of the loan.

Lenders and borrowers in the open banking model praise this new model of banking. Lenders are able to earn a higher rate than from a standard savings account, while borrowers pay less per payment than on a credit card. Secondly, users like the interaction with a community of "real" people as opposed to a faceless entity, like a bank. In other words, open banking is a form of social networking, indicating a huge potential to attract the Millennial group, which likely needs credit and whose members already spend much time logged onto social networking sites (e.g., Facebook, Flickr).

Although the platform itself is not difficult to create, the question for banks is where the value is for the profit margin, and how the change in a bank's relationship with its customers will affect the bottom line. The questions are worth pondering since open banking will drive the financial industry towards a different definition of a bank's core business functions and competencies, as well as shift the bank's role to one of trusted advisor from that of the guardian of funds.

## 10 Mashups

Mashups are part of the Web 2.0 solar system, as described earlier. Defined on Wikipedia as "a website or web application that seamlessly combines content from more than one source into an integrated experience," mashups offer a compelling alternative to proprietary applications. Mashup developers source the content for a mashup from an open application programming interface (API) of such online companies as Google and Yahoo!, which have made their APIs open. The requisite features from each API are then mixed together in order to create a new, and sometimes better, application. Mashups generally address specific needs.

There are a growing number of mashups online. Some are purely for entertainment, such as Podbop, which allows users to search for visiting bands to a specific zip code in the United States. Other mashups are more practical, such as HousingMaps.com, which finds out where homes are listed for sale in the San Francisco area and then plots them immediately on a Google Map.

Business models for monetizing and capitalizing on mashups are not yet concrete. However, commercial interest is growing in mashups, with companies seeing a huge potential for highly targeted advertising as well as other profitable applications. For example, an advertising mashup could generate online ads that may be targeted not only according to keyword search, but also to a person's specific location.

Venture capitalist Peter Rip defines mashup-as-business (MAB) as one that actually creates value beyond the value created by the original sources. In order for a mashup to be successful as an MAB, it could become the owner of new proprietary data, new proprietary logic, proprietary process or even a combination of the three. The problem with developing new proprietary data is that the cost is high; the problem with proprietary process or logic is that the customer process is relatively simple, making the addition of value particularly difficult. Ultimately, the data owner is in control. If the data owner decides to block information in any way, the mashup, which requires data feeds, would run into trouble.

Mashup applications can potentially provide banks with a flexible and low-cost platform to furnish customized services to the individual customer. These applications offer customers a social networking experience, which adds to the user experience, making them feel important, and ultimately helping the bank to retain its customers more easily.

One day Daniel, Wil and I drove up a mountain to talk to Jaron Lanier, a guru according to Daniel. He said meeting him was a super opportunity that we shouldn't miss. The door was opened by a big man in bare feet and his hair in enormous dreadlocks; he had a surprisingly soft voice. We were led through a house packed with impressions and stories from his life to a big room full of octopuses. In the twilight of the late afternoon, it felt like we ended up in a big aquarium. Sitting on his opium bed, Jaron talked for many intriguing hours about the complexity and developments in ICT, so many stories and impressions that I thought my head would burst with ICT.

Margreet Oostenbrink

Chapter 6

# Interviews: Consultations with the experts

Worldwide interviews with a range of experts, representing specific fields, are an integral part of the process to define the driving forces. A core team of participants met with 30 dynamic and influential authorities to gather fresh perspectives and new insights that helped shape the team's understanding of the key drivers in the landscape. The experts were:

- Ton van Asseldonk
- Henk Badoux & Richard Dingemans
- David Bank
- Eddy Bex
- Michiel Boreel
- Natarajan Chandrasekaran
- Peter Cochrane
- Victor d'Alfonso
- Jack van Driel
- Deepak Ghaisas
- Christian Goeckenjan & Richard Lowrie
- Ashwin Goyal
- Eric van Heck
- Theo Huibers
- Brewster Kahle
- Heikki Karjaluoto
- Jongwan Kim
- Vivek Kulkarni
- Praveen Kumar
- Jaron Lanier
- Peter Leyden
- Krish Murali Eswar
- Eric Rodenbeck
- Ralph Schonenback & Severin Weiss
- Rajeev Srivastava
- Fred Studer
- Anthony Townsend
- Eddy Vermeire

A select number of interviews are summarised and presented in this section. Any errors or inaccuracies that appear in these summaries are the sole responsibility of the DTN.

# Ton van Asseldonk

Founder, TVA Development BV



Ton van Asseldonk's work as a consultant takes him through processes to understand how people can organise for an unpredictable world. From his observations and study, he has seen many companies stretch their traditional business processes beyond what was thought to be possible, shifting from "the massive heterogeneity in consumer markets to the complete matter of unpredictability of individual, moment-specific, client behaviour. One-size-fits-all solutions have become obsolete, and every client has become individual. This means that companies must alter their processes, which were originally push-oriented, towards more p47 p73 consumer-driven processes." He argues that this move is inevitable because of the inefficiencies of push-oriented processes, which generate mounting costs. Industrial processes must give way to more consumer-driven processes. He illustrates his argument by comparing the car industry with a retail clothing manufacturer, Benetton. The car industry can only start manufacturing at the time when the client's demand is known. It only takes six hours to actually assemble the car, but it takes three months for the client to receive it because of the three months required to organise the different processes of transporting the car from the factory to the client. By comparison, Benetton has reversed the sequence of events in its supply chain. Traditionally, the wool is dyed first before the knitting process. However, this entails knowing exactly what colours will sell before knitting—a difficult prediction to make. Benetton has now reversed the process, knitting before dyeing the clothing, which enables the company to serve the market as soon as the colours change.

p49 p75 Van Asseldonk predicts that banks will soon face a highly competitive market. In much the same way as Voice-over-IP (VoIP) changed the telephone market, banks will need to change their business model as the world realises that there is too much money and too few people who know what to do with it. Profit margins for banks are shrinking and their traditional role is disappearing. In van Asseldonk's view, banks have been money-pushers and not service providers, such that the concept of service in the banking sector has not yet matured.

He predicts that in the future the value of banking will be in providing private banking products and services for the masses. He perceives the needs of regular individuals as being relatively the same as those of wealthier individuals, but on a smaller scale; and the banks have not found ways to provide advisory services to these potential small investors. His concept of a sound strategic model is one that includes private banking for everyone at industrial cost parity—a future he envisions to be developing naturally soon. To some degree, van Asseldonk believes that "the bank has actually split itself up into microbanks because every specific

## *"There's too much money, and we know too little what to do with it—so, it's worthless."*

loan to every specific client becomes, in effect, a bank in its own right." Not only will there be private banking for everyone, but there may no longer be a need for a banking institution. The value is no longer just the money. As trust wears thinner, financial advice and security as a service will add value to the banking business.

Van Asseldonk speaks of a prevailing attitude of the industry to focus the business around the bank and not around its clients, preventing banks from creating "client value." This culture or mental attitude could be changed if banks were to "organise their own opposition": bringing clients in for discussions about a variety of options. Failing that, banks run the risk of stagnation or moving too slowly to save the business. He sees ICT as an agent for "catalyzing energy, whatever that energy is." Therefore, the role of ICT departments in banks is to develop the platform to bring about this needed change. Although building these communities is difficult, the strengthening of personal contacts will ultimately benefit the bank by enabling it to gather better client information. By successfully managing the relationships, the bank can generate a higher level of trust, a critical factor in successful banking relationships. If banks could develop a capability for translating client requirements, providing instruments for obtaining this information, they could get smarter information with more time-saving for the client—time being a bigger scarcity in the world than money.

Van Asseldonk expresses fears about data security. If a bank is broken down into an "endless sea of microbanks," there needs to be an infrastructure and system in place to ensure the correctness of the data, and the possibility for aggregation at any level. If the data is not embedded somewhere in the process, data integrity is not secured. The bank would be given to making decisions based on corrupt data, and thus be vulnerable to considerable problems "because [its] virtual image of the online reality is not a true representation of reality anymore."

The concept of a local bank is in flux, with the blurring of geographical limits. Territorial connections no longer necessarily reflect geographical maps as the world gets more interconnected and interdependent. "There is no point in creating a local bank based on a geographical definition if the geographical dimension is becoming less and less important," he says. However, banks should not be too quick to dismiss that geographical limits are a basic parameter and will not change because "there are sufficient examples of companies in the past who have been wiped out by sudden changes of the basic parameters on which the business would run."

customer-driven | client unpredictability | mass private banking | Van Asseldonk

OUTSOURCING
VIRTUAL
RESPECT
OPEN
GET A GRIP
You can RELY on me.
Who are my CUSTOMERS?

If we would only have known that hunting gorillas/finding uncertainties would involve watching more than 30 hours of video interviews with people from all over the world ... but the richness of new viewpoints, some of them radical, others of the “why-didn’t-we-think-of-that-before-ourselves” verity made it an inspiring workshop.

Mark Hese

Henk Badoux

# Henk Badoux & Richard Dingemans

Director Banking Solution CRM, SAP; Business Consultant, SAP

Richard Dingemans and Henk Badoux speak about the impact of Internet banking, the need for a service-oriented banking architecture, the importance of structure to ICT security, and innovation. To the banking customer, the Internet gives the perception that transactions can take place whenever and wherever. The customer is no longer limited to the official banking hours in order to conduct basic transactions, such as money transfers. However, the downside of this development is a deterioration of customer service in banks—so much so that customers do not receive any real attention and a variety of procedures are now up to the customer to figure out and accomplish on his/her own. Technology is necessary for cutting costs; however, in an increasingly competitive environment, banks need to find a way to reconnect with their customers so that service at the branch is as receptive and user-friendly as through the Internet.

Not all countries have a strong service orientation in their businesses. But, "it is important to have a person who will deliver the right response when a customer calls up." One way to fill the need is to outsource the bank's call centre to countries where people have a cultural inclination to provide quality service, and to train these service providers in the parent company's language. CRM systems on their own will not solve the current issues of banking; the customer's emotional response to service is seen to be vastly more significant. Because managing customer data becomes problematic without it, ICT remains a major prerequisite for the banking environment.

Over the next 10 years, Dingemans and Badoux see the necessity for establishing a service-oriented architecture with larger applications split into smaller components. The smaller components can then be used to build the process. Thus, more business can be done efficiently and flexibly. To the question of whether vendors of large-scale systems, such as Oracle and SAP can innovate as nimbly as younger and smaller developers given the emergence of open source, Dingemans and Badoux believe these entities simply cannot allow themselves to be resistant to innovation; that improvements will result from demands for compliance and customer innovation.

Dingemans and Badoux stress the importance of structure to avert hacking by external sources. Because the collapse of a large bank will seriously undermine the economy, there p58 p65 is a need for structure in banks to ensure security. A caveat to this is the need for flexibility and room for organisation in order for projects and processes to accommodate needed modifications.

# *"The most important question is— will innovation happen from within a system or from without?"*

Regarding the traditional characteristic of the financial services sector to be conservative and slow to change, the pair stress the positive impact of bringing in new knowledge. Whether it comes from somewhere within the industry or from without is a primary consideration. While a fresh perspective from a different industry may add some value, it is more likely that new knowledge will come from a younger generation within the same industry. The speakers believe that innovation in renewing existing landscape and architecture will go through an evolutionary process, not a revolutionary one.

DAVID BANK
Reporter/Wall Street Journal
Senior VP/Civic Ventures NFP
RABOBANK
I've paid my dues, now I'm out to ENJOY!
The EFFECTS of AGING on SOCIETY & FINANCIAL INSTITUTIONS
Can we turn the AGING POPULATION trend into an OPPORTUNITY instead of a CRISIS?
• retirement lasts 30-40 yrs
• labour shortage
• rising health care costs
• inventing A NEW STAGE of LIF
"ABBEY's" = AGING
"RAPPEYS" = RICH &
¿ ORACLE QUESTION ?
How could we bring VOLUNTEERISM into SPOTLIGHT?
• clash of OLDER WHITE population needing HEALTH CARE and YOUNG LATINOS needing SCHOOLING
What new FORMS of VALUE will be born that BANKS can support
and DEVELOP?
Bank managing NEW RELATIONSHIPS
We've got the POWER now
THE (technology) CUSTOMER REVOLT
CUSTOMERS
■ "PERMEABLE" DIVISION between work and retirement
→ WHAT'S THE FINANCIAL SOLUTION?
■ PRICING re-balanced
■ BREAKING away from LOCK-IN technologies
■ OPEN SOURCE adds weight in negotiations
Yeah, I'm keeping my options 'OPEN'
■ Developing "TIME DOLLARS"
1h
"EDUCATION EUROS"
BOTTOM
TECHNOLOGY
■ enabling
require
VOLUNTE
■ Developing a new BALANCE SHEET with POSITIVE & NEGATIVE EXTERNALITIES
PARADIGM SHIFT needed
■ SOCIAL ENTREPRENE is on the RIS
Doesn't exactly HELP my QUARTERLY RESULTS to look any BETTER, does it?
Someone has to take the 1ST BRAVE STEP
TEACH someone to READ today,
SAVE on JAIL COSTS in the next 15 yrs

LIFE-SPAN
FINANCIAL MGMT
& ADVICE
We need INNOVATION in how we approach the issue
Should & could we take on a BIGGER ROLE from
the SOCIETY'S PERSPECTIVE?
breaking THROUGH the inhibiting BUREAUCRACY
BUT WE STILL
YOUR BUSINESS!
SHHHH!
BANKS to manage HUMAN CAPITAL, too?
SOCIAL INVESTMENT
SECURITY
Who's RESPONSIBLE?
You need us, the BIG VENDOR, to ensure
your DATA SAFETY!
FEAR is the most EFFECTIVE WAY to GAIN CONTROL

# David Bank

**SVP, Civic Ventures and Director, Civic Ventures Institute**

A former journalist for the *Wall Street Journal,* covering technology, David Bank made the switch to a nonprofit social entrepreneurship where he could deliver a major promise of technology: its utility in solving social problems. Rather than write about technology, Bank opted to become directly involved in solving social problems through the use of technology.

Bank talks about "customer revolt" and trends in the software industry that have strengthened customer negotiations with vendors.p73 Large and small customers are increasingly active in trying to gain independence from their vendors. Bank points out two drivers for this development: product pricing, and technology lock-in and standards. Customers were able to gain steep discounts from vendors on the order of 90% from the list prices. It showed that the price structure of the software industry is in fact more advantageous to customers than vendors wanted customers to know. Regarding technology lock-in and standards, the industry has long been moving towards openness, interoperability and interconnections, allowing customers more choice of products and brands. These developments have triggered the emergence of a viable open-source stack that Bank believes will be valuable as an option to help with vendor negotiations and keep them "honest both on pricing and on the adherence to these technology standards." While customers are thus empowered for negotiating with vendors, the question remains how to institutionalize the trend and keep it going.

Addressing system integration, Bank agrees that the different systems of an organisation should all be able to talk to one another so that there is one coherent view of the customer.p58 What transpires at the back end, etc., is a way for an organisation to understand customers better as well as to hold all processes from the supply chain, inventory, fulfillment, etc. If the integration is provided by a single vendor, the vendor can be expected to supply not only the technology, but in a sense, also supply the company's business model. While implementation is difficult and integration is thought to bring more headaches than benefits, system integration is expected to become easier as interfaces and programming standards become more standardised. The process of integration will be aided by other trends, such as outsource developments and cheaper programming resources. According to Bank, open source keeps these standards open and helps to enforce them, acting as a driver in facilitating system integration.

Bank sees aging as a trend effecting changes in the economic dynamics of the world and predicts that it will soon change our ideas about retirement. In the last several decades, as young people entered the workforce, older workers have been crowded out or pushed

*"John Gardner said: 'Society faces unprecedented opportunities disguised as insolvable problems.'"*

to retire earlier and earlier. Marketing and economic arrangements reinforced the course by encouraging people to enjoy early retirement. However, in recent years, the trend has changed, prompted by looming labour shortages: engineers, teachers, nurses, etc. Additionally, the Baby Boomers are on the brink of retirement, raising the spectre of a small workforce burdened with support for an overwhelming number of retirees. As people continue to live longer, their retirement period is extended; and expectations are that it will become much longer, and, consequently, more expensive. While the retirement age is set at 65, people now live well into their 80s, 90s and beyond, indicating 30 to 50 years of retirement. Bank believes that current notions about aging and retirement will change. He predicts that they are "due for a major upheaval, in terms of individual attitudes towards retirement, corporate attitudes towards older workers, and government policies about retirement finance, and the effect it is going to have on their budgets."

Bank refers to a new age group made up of people approximately 55 to 75 years of age. The group has not been identified by name, and its social meaning has yet to be fully explored. However, the common characteristics of this age group are noted by Bank. They "want to stay involved, are engaged and active, and have an, immense reservoir of talent and experience." Having spent most of their lives working or attending to the practical details of living, part of this cohort will see retirement as a chance to accomplish personal goals, dreams they have harboured in their earlier years to make a social contribution. For others whose financial situation in retirement is insecure or unstable—because of insufficient savings, failing government or corporate pension schemes, etc.—the need to continue working will be very real. Bank believes that the combination of these trends—the coming of this new stage of life, the development of a new set of work arrangements, and the emergence of a new set of financial arrangements around this new period of life—presents an immense opportunity for people to "work at what they want to work at, make some more money to shore up their retirement with finances, and save the world at the same time."

The development can trigger innovation in the banking sector by generating demand for "new kinds of value flows and new kinds of financing mechanisms." Since they already provide retirement planning, etc., banks and financial services institutions would generally be well-positioned to meet these demands. This would effectively expand the banking sector's currently limited financial role into broader life-planning functions, giving banks a deeper relationship with their customers.

Bank offers two possible scenarios to address whether such changes will actually take place, and what might occur if they do. In the worse scenario there is generational warfare. The better scenario envisions a win-win situation. Attitudes would change for the better with support from government and NGOs, and a way is forged for older generations to lend a helping hand to younger generations, allowing the former to play a mentoring role in return for help with their own retirement. It would then be entirely possible for people to have another career after their primary career. Referring to some of the possibilities, Bank suggests careers in social entrepreneurship schemes: using time-shares, retirees live out their golden years in beautiful, exotic countries where the cost of living is low, and simultaneously put their talents and experience to work in partnerships with local communities. p48 Bank sees more and more of this kind of bottom-up social entrepreneurship emerging worldwide. He stresses, however, that policies and attitudes towards the notion of pensions and second careers need to change. In the United States, for example, the practice is considered "double dipping" and is generally frowned upon. Bank argues that double dipping is actually part of the social solution: on top of their pensions, retirees continue to earn a small income that allows them a good living for a few more years, and younger generations benefit from their experience and wisdom.

Bank emphasizes that social arrangements will work only within a certain time frame, after which the dynamics change and a new social arrangement is needed to replace the old structure. Demographics are influential in driving these changes, as evidenced by the impact of the Baby Boomer generation on almost every industry sector, on government policies, etc.

On the subject of open source technologies and the prevailing perception that they threaten the bottom line, Bank argues that open source actually "enables a new wave of innovation, investment and mobilisation on the technology." Citing the example of the Internet, he recalls that it was initially seen as a threat to many software companies. But, as it turned out, it actually became the industry's biggest boon. Although open source is currently seen as the next big threat to software companies, Bank is assured that with continuous innovation and growth, "the spread and the democratisation of the technology should turn out to be a huge economic win for companies, as well as private investors generally."

The issue of security in open source—a question particularly pertinent to the banking sector—is an ongoing concern and remains unresolved. Those who argue that open source

*"The trend is towards integration of systems; single-vendor implementations have run its course."*

is more secure point out that most of the vulnerabilities are actually caused by software bugs, and the fault lies with vendors who are generally slow in fixing them. Those who are less sure about the security of open source contend that if one can openly read the source code, then one can be much more ahead of the game in finding and taking advantage of the weaknesses. However, Bank suggests that making a distinction between open source and proprietary technology is not a sound basis for choosing between the two options. In the end, the decision must be supported by the belief that open source is better, more secure, more robust and cheaper.

Interviews are a powerful tool to produce new insights within the organisation. By stating clear and strong opinions, the interviewees force us to review and reshape our own opinions.

Sjaak Oosterveer

# Eddy Bex

CIO, Fin-Force



As the CIO of Fin-Force, Eddy Bex is responsible for ICT infrastrucutre. While the data centre activity of the company is outsourced, Bex retains overall responsibility for software maintenance and development of new applications. As the CIO, he understands the importance of software packages and the need to implement structure that is actually supported by the package itself, rather than change the package to accommodate the organisation's own structure. Outsourcing is a recurring theme in Bex's interview, as are the issues inherent in outsourcing and its potential benefits.

Despite its current popularity Bex finds that outsourcing does not lend itself to the success of projects, and addresses some of its downsides. Bex suggests that "the amount of attention from the project point of view, project management, communication and coordination point of view, that you have to put in an offshoring or a near-shoring activity is so extreme that so far people have not been able to manage that quite sufficiently correctly, unless it is concerning projects that are really straightforward, like the Euro conversion in the year 2000." Outsourcing is an option when an organisation's requirements and the activities involved are straightforward. However, Bex is optimistic that some time in the future, someone will discover the most productive model for working with distant locations; and notes that, cost-wise, outsourcing is, in reality, an option that cannot be ignored.

He also notes that in the last five years, rates for outsourcing contracts have steadily risen, which could possibly eliminate the need for outsourcing in the future. Whether or not the rates will rise to the level where it is no longer cost-effective, Bex believes that, ultimately, the business requirement side will remain where customers are located.

Bex shared his views on project management and ICT, noting that, in the past, project cycles in software development were relatively short and projects were completed within a span p76 of six to nine months. However, in the past, project management or project management capabilities were not as well structured or supported by complete methodologies as they are today. Instead, the success of a project was determined by the knowledge and the capabilities of the people involved. The result was that a project could be done successfully once, but had a much lower chance of having the same level of success in subsequent rounds. In order to correct this vulnerability, project management was introduced. However, project management can over formalize the process, and methodologies on the software development side were more or less neglected. Thus, there is a pendulum-swing in finding the right

*"Outsourcing could move towards selling mortgage processes rather than single services."*



balance between software development project management and its methodologies. Bex uses the example to express caution about letting the same series of events happen on the project life cycle. He has seen it extended from six or nine months to 15 months, and expresses concern that if project duration were to stretch even further, ICT costs would then become too prohibitive and the organisation would fail to realise its business case. Beck considers the project life cycle to have become very expensive and time-consuming and believes it is time to shorten the cycle with the help of project management tools and methodologies that have matured and evolved.

Bex indicats concern about loss of knowledge in the ICT sector, regarding this as a growing problem, made worse by new and changing technology. The sector faces the threat from having retired 70%-90% of its workforce in the past 15 years. It was once possible to quickly find people who could answer questions: "By asking the right questions, we could give you the information you needed in order to help you design your systems." As people who had a lifetime of experience in the ICT sector are no longer active in the business, Bex suggests that an approach be developed that will enable everyone to obtain that knowledge.

He admits that because of growing complexity in the market, specialisation will be key in keeping a handle on the process of knowledge management. New organisations will enter the market to address specific knowledge needs. In the banking industry, the trend for specialisation is already happening with the increasing emergence of small organisations and their success in bringing new business.

According to Bex, a bank should not enter the process outsourcing business as a standalone activity, but consider instead its relationship to the company's global ICT architecture and how process outsourcing fits into it. If not, the bank risks serious consequences. He reasons that a company's main business may change over the course of the next several years, and its global ICT architecture must continue to keep its ability to support the organisation's relationship with clients. For banks, managing customer information is now a core activity, and a bank's business is to manage clients well and ensure that they have more and more products and services to offer. Architecturally, a solid infrastructure must be in place to support the process and to disseminate shareable client information. "You need the capability of talking to your customers; you need the capability of determining what your strategy is, what is it that business-wise makes sense for your organisation, and the capability of putting that on paper, in order to start working based on that and detailing it out." The role of ICT will change to support such client management activity. ICT will have to become "the glue"—from a technical point of view—between the bank and the service organisations."

Bex draws distinctions between outsourcing for ICT and outsourcing for business processes. Defining the requirements is the basis for any outsourcing contract, whether for ICT outsourcing or for business process. The organisation that will provide outsourcing services should know what the expectations and business requirements of the contractor are. The next level of business process outsourcing (BPO) will involve more cooperative work between the sending organisation and the receiving organisation. What can be outsourced is very limited, but there is a prevailing assumption that the organisation engaged for outsourcing has the proper capabilities from a business and process management point of view. Bex believes ICT outsourcing is different. For this, the organisation needs to accept the actual software. By comparison, in BPO, the acceptability of the level or quality of service is a key consideration. It is about whether or not the payment is executed in time and toward the right channel. For ICT outsourcing, it is about the acceptance of the developed software and whether it will enable the organisation to execute the payment itself within a certain timeframe. In another difference between the two, BPO is a service that the organisation receives, and must continuously manage and improve its quality.

IT outsourcing is often a one-time affair as far as a solution is concerned. From a knowledge perspective, BPO requires strategic consideration, whereas ICT outsourcing requires more in-depth knowledge. Because of the complexity of managing the ICT outsourcing process, an architecture must be created in order to "plug and play" software components in order to manage this complexity and keep it within reasonable limits.

Generally, the financial sector is very traditional and conservative. There is a tendency to "do it all, keep it all in-house, and be in charge of our own belly." Unlike other industry sectors, banks and other financial institutions have a valuable asset in their relationship with clients. While this was a source of competitive advantage in the past, the relationship is becoming more and more fluid. Customers are no longer as loyal, thus weakening the ties between the bank and its clients. Bex believes the banks are at risk of losing these relationships, which are their only real assets, if they do not focus on keeping them alive.

# *"Outsourcing won't be just about costs, but about entire business processes."*

Commenting on the ongoing process of the European Commission to establish a single market ("Europeanisation movement"), Bex finds the financial sector under tremendous pressure. It must comply with a series of new legislation, new changes and new products involved in creating the new European marketplace.

Sharing his views on the open technology movement, Bex expresses his preference as CIO for open technology to prove its viability before making an investment in it. He believes p47 that, to some degree, the service must be guaranteed. Although open technology and open systems can be expected to replace a slowly disappearing mainframe environment and become the new status quo, Bex expresses concern about when this might happen and whether a company can achieve the same maintenance and availability figures as with mainframe environments.

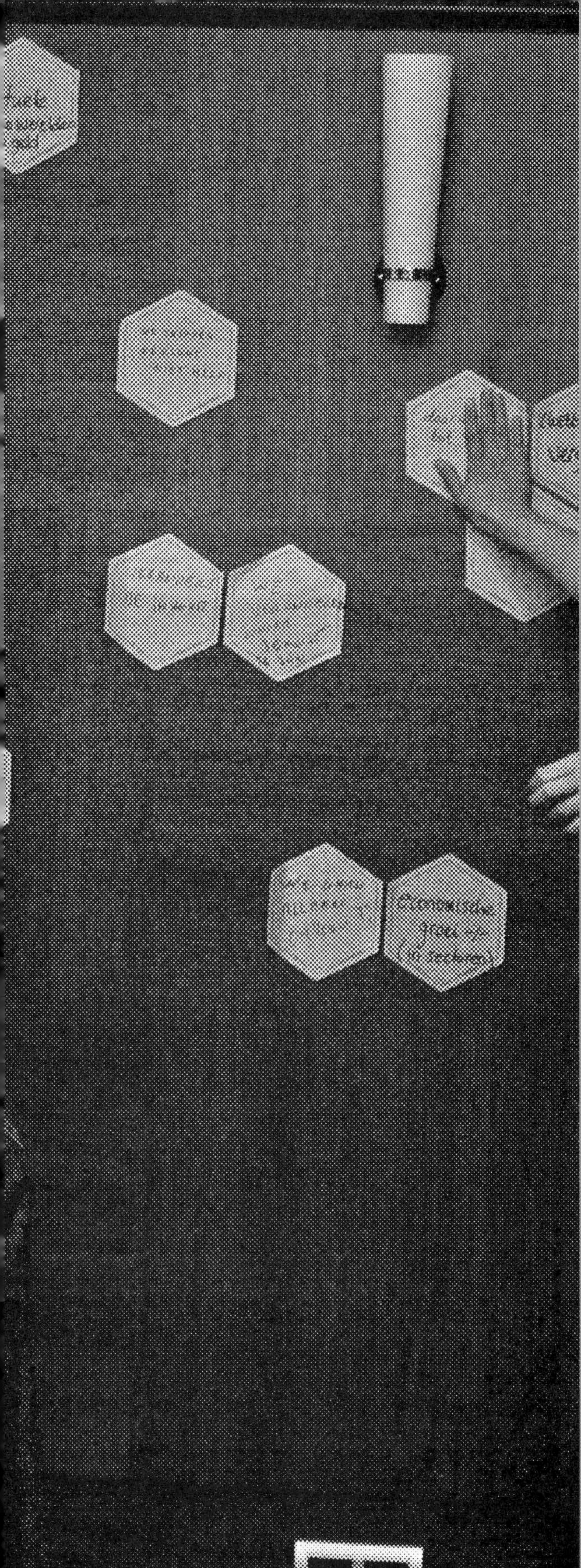

The amount of information from interviews and research was overwhelming. It was unbelievable to see that, with the right techniques and visualisations, this could all be taken in within two days in such a way we would even remember most of it afterwards.

Rob Bakker

# Michiel Boreel

## Director of Strategy, Sogeti Think Tank

As the Director of Strategy for Sogeti, Michiel Boreel is primarily responsible for developing a strategy for customer service and for research and publication. A specialist in ICT, he is a published author and an acknowledged expert on the industry. In the interview, Boreel shares his thoughts on the ICT industry and where the industry is going.

Dismissing the common usage of the term "maturing industry" for the ICT sector, Boreel states that the phrase is more applicable for describing a phase of the industry cycle. He describes the industry cycle as composed of different stages, alternately characterized by innovation, growth, maturation, consolidation and stablisation. The ICT industry has matured and has been in the stabilisation/consolidation phase of the cycle in the last four or five years, and is poised for a new growth phase. Supporting this belief, Boreel refers to the growing importance of accountability as an issue in ICT over the last five years. Due partly to an emphasis on compliance and corporate governance, a sharpening focus on accountability is to be seen as a sign of maturation in the ICT industry: "It is like a child attaining adolescence and then maturing by realising that he has to be [held] accountable for things [that he does] or the decisions that he makes."

After the dot.com boom-bust period, there was a lot of pessimism regarding the benefits that ICT could deliver. However, Boreel now sees a shift once again to optimism with people believing that ICT is a very important driving force in generating productivity and efficiency. For Boreel, ICT should not be seen simply as a burden or a cost factor. Instead, it is once more a rewarding investment for reducing costs and creating new revenue channels, new relationships with customers and new values. He finds it interesting that the shift is driven by customers themselves. Illustrating the power of bottom-up processes, Boreel offers a personal anecdote of a motto he saw on a T-shirt at an open source seminar: "Never underestimate the p48 power of dumb people in large groups."[*] He advocates the adoption of this motto by financial institutions, suggesting that if they can use technology as a new medium to organise a new form of bottom-up media, financial institutions will benefit in the long run.

According to Boreel, an effect of bottom-up processes is that they will challenge conventional wisdom and prove it wrong, and new truths will be examined and appraised. Bottom-up media will also change the traditional notions of trust, particularly in the financial services industry. A bank conducts business on the basis of trust established between it and its clients: Customers use a bank they can trust, and that trust is built upon a bank's performance, which can just as easily destroy that trust. Bottom-up media will change how banks build trust.

# *"You can only outsource things that you have stabilised."*



Boreel refers to the concept of consumer or customer advocacy, which assumes the knowledge consumers have about their bank: that it is doing its best for its customers. p74 This can be promoted by involving the customer at all levels of the bank's activities, by transforming the business, moving from product creation and pushing them on customers to inviting them to participate in the process of product and service innovations.

Boreel sees at least two opposing sides in technology that can affect ICT departments: people who believe that technology is there for the betterment of human life; and those who believe that technology actually makes life worse. Boreel refers to the latter as "techno-pessimists." In order to address techno-pessimists, ICT departments in financial institutions must be able to present ICT in such a way that it is not thought of as technology. The user interface and the process must become very simple, cheap, easily accessible and ubiquitous, so that working with technology becomes as natural as breathing. Whether or not this can be accomplished will in the end depend upon the customer's trust in the bank that the shift towards using increasingly ICT-dependent processes will yield the same sound results.

On the issue of ICT outsourcing, Boreel views ICT not as a commodity but as a platform to connect with customers and, therefore, is strongly linked with a company's business processes. However, in situations where ICT has been standardised, and is therefore a commodity, it may be outsourced relatively easily. These two aspects of ICT suggest that it can partly be a commodity that can be managed, stabilised and outsourced; and partly as an activity that needs to be kept in-house. He outlined three primary areas that absolutely should not be outsourced. The brains or the technical architecture—even for outsourced products or processes—should be kept in-house. The connection between ICT and business, or the elements and processes where ICT adds value to the business, should also not be outsourced. Nor should the governance of the actual contract be outsourced; the bank must ensure for itself that the contractual arrangements are actually delivered.

Boreel sees a major problem in ICT outsourcing in that it suggests "a simplicity or standardisation/stabilisation of technology that is just not there." A second problem is that technology moves in booms and busts. Thus, when technology is outsourced, the organisation risks being limited to a bursting bubble. If all ICT activities are outsourced to a vendor to reduce costs, then there is a real risk of the company being hampered from taking advantage of and thriving on new technological breakthroughs.

After ICT moves past its growth and innovation phase and into a stabilisation/consolidation phase, Boreel believes it becomes much easier to use packaged solutions. Although standard solutions are now available, he notes that taking parts out of a present system and replacing them with something else is problematic, because not all interfaces are standardised. This requires "designing systems from an architecture that actually standardises interfaces, so [that] it becomes easier to replace them."

Boreel predicts that banking itself will become increasingly complex. To become customer advocates, banks will need to be very creative, adjusting products and services not simply to a group or groups of customers, but also to the individual customer. Complexity will arise from the need to provide mass customisation at a level where the bank can still turn a profit. This picture is rendered even more complex by the understanding that there are no one-size-fits-all solutions. Banks will need to be very flexible and very fast in order to create and bring new products to market in a very short time.

Boreel questions whether banks can move from pushing products to supporting customers. Changing customer behaviour is prompting banks to move towards a future where the shift will become a necessity. Customer loyality is steadily declining with the increasing number of product options and different players in the financial sector. Competition is intensifying across the sector, and all the players will need to anticipate this imperative by understanding and responding to the changing needs of their customers. Boreel stresses that customer loyalty is driven more by feelings that the company is doing what is best for them, rather than by other factors, such as best prices, cheap products, etc. Therefore, a bank's brand is the promise of performance that the bank will do what is in the best interest of its customers.

Sharing his views on Rabobank, Boreel expresses his belief that the bank is in a better position than its competitors. It has a long-established corporate culture of doing what is best for its customers; and of regarding profit as not the only thing that matters. Boreel suggests that the challenge for Rabobank will be to leverage this culture and transform it to fit "modern society with modern media and modern technology." The future role of the bank's ICT department will be to make the Rabobank systems stable, efficient, less costly, reliable, simple and easy to use, rather than to create competitive advantage.

The interviews opened our eyes in many ways. First we saw gorillas emerging from the mist where we never expected them. Once a gorilla was identified you would see it everywhere around you in the daily work. What is great is that obtained insights stay. They are still useful in my new job.

Jeanne Driessen

# Natarajan Chandrasekaran

## Executive Vice President and Head of Global Operations, Tata Consultancy Services

Having been with Tata Consultancy Services (TCS) for more than 19 years, Natarajan Chandrasekaran has been a front-row observer of the changes that took place in the ICT sector over the last 10 years. He lists four major developments that have shaped the present:

- The likelihood of the total replacement of mainframes by client/server;
- The threat of Y2K incompatibility;
- The Internet; and
- Global sourcing.

Technologically, much has happened over the last 10 years, not the least of which is the emergence of India as an ICT superpower. However, Chandrasekaran warns that it is difficult to determine whether a technology will succeed or fail. For technologies to be successful and widely adopted, they must also "stand the test of performance, scalability and security, among other things." This is the main reason that many technologies fail to hit the mark despite the substantial promise they displayed before the launch.

In the face of increasing complexity and a simultaneous rise in demand for simplicity, Chandrasekaran suggests that the role of ICT departments, as system integrators, is to p58 simplify this complexity.* ICT management, Chandrasekaran predicts, is going to be one of the most complex jobs, requiring not only ICT skills, but also business acumen. Global sourcing will place mounting pressure on knowledge and talent retention in ICT departments everywhere. Technological changes, the availability of the Internet and its relevance in emerging markets will cause disruptive changes in business models for corporations. However, Chandrasekaran is optimistic that as long as the complexities are recognised, the new situation can be managed efficiently, albeit differently.

He believes that global demand for talent is going to increase exponentially. The supply-demand gap for knowledge and talent will further widen. Because of heightened mobility, corporations will also experience a "talent leakage." However, Chandrasekaran expects that highly sophisticated collaborative tools will emerge in the marketplace that will try to leverage talent across the globe, thereby alleviating the problem of talent shortage.

Predicting the integration of ICT and corporate operations in the near future, Chandrasekaran shares his optimism for this outcome. Currently run as two independent units, he believes

*"Any outsourcing or offshoring, leveraging the global workforce, must have reasons beyond production costs."*



that greater collaboration between the two would "bring about tremendous digitisation opportunities for processes that will drive efficiencies." ICT has the potential to eliminate many of the intermediate tasks and to resolve issues in real time rather than to go through cases sequentially. Furthermore, ICT can be leveraged to give business analyses with real-time information and identify patterns in the data and reduce complexity.

Chandrasekaran sees India and China as important suppliers of global talent. Considering the demographics of the graduates and the quality of education, India and China are seen to be making rapid progress, rising through the ranks of emerging countries to compete with the West. However, Chandrasekaran notes that China is at a disadvantage in its demographic profile. China's population is rapidly aging, whereas approximately 54% of India's population is under 23 years of age. With this young talent and energy, India will be more competitive than China in the long run. He further believes that India is poised for the next level of growth. To date, most of India's success has been in "servicing global corporations, in terms of system development, system maintenance and all the related work." He predicts that the next phase will lie in the creation of intellectual property. Many small companies in India have entered a particular niche and come up with very innovative solutions. The confluence of an energetic, youthful workforce and a strong entrepreneurial spirit will drive this revolution.

On the topic of outsourcing, Chandrasekaran cautions that it must be done for reasons beyond production costs. With India as one of the primary recipients of outsourcing contracts, his words carry the weight of first-hand knowledge and observation: "If it is done purely for cost reasons, it will not be a small thing in the long term, even if it is considered tactical at some point in time." Citing a right reason for outsourcing, he suggests that it should be undertaken for "achieving a superior ICT architecture and a superior value of ICT to the business." If this is understood to be the goal, the role of ICT can be accepted in terms of operational excellence and business innovation. When understood by both parties to the contract, the partner will be "empowered to make a significant contribution as an extension of the company" and ensure the success of the outsourcing process. While there is a cost advantage for Western companies to outsource now, Chandrasekaran acknowledges that wages are on the rise across India, and in the future, it will be important to realise other benefits such as process improvement, quality and time to market. On the labour market for ICT professionals, he notes that global demand is on the rise. The number of ICT professionals in the West is declining, whereas the numbers are increasing in India and China. He expects the shortage in the West to be met by ICT professionals from these emerging economies. This will raise questions about reforms: what kinds of reforms are necessary to enable the countries to capture the rising demand, and what critical skills are needed to fulfill the demand?

Explaining why India has become a recognised success in the outsourcing service industry, Chandrasekaran points to the strong background India has in mathematics and logical p73 analysis and its complex cultural environment.* India is a country of great diversity with many different languages, cultures and religions. Its people live in a highly complex and chaotic environment. For Chandrasekaran, this inborn ability of Indians to handle complexity may be a reason for the country's success.

Sharing his thoughts on open source, Chandrasekaran seems sure that the phenomenon will play a dominant role in the future. For large-scale systems, the only factors that will deter open source are performance and security. If open source is available to everybody, then the governance of open source advancements will become an important issue. He also foresees pressure to create secure systems in open source. While legacy systems will not disappear entirely, he expects that questions about component replacement and integration could be an issue: "There is no magic source to replace everything."

PETER COCHRANE
Former CTO / BT
RABOBANK
FUTUREVISION
The MAGIC MOBILE will CUT YOU DOWN!
BANK, Walk with ME!
TECHNOLOGIAL REVOLUTION is waiting to happen
PROVIDING VALUE instead of PRODUCTS
USING CUSTOMER INFORMATION TO CREATE CUSTOMER BENEFITS
NOW
BANK
TRUE
I'm AN INDUSTRY!
NO, YOU'RE SUPPOSED TO PROVIDE SERVICE!
OPEN 9:30-16:00 MON-FRI
Why don't you SPEAK MY LANGUAGE?
DON'T ASK HOW MUCH I'LL PAY YOU, ASK WHAT YOU CAN DO FOR ME!
BUT I NEED HELP NOW!
Need for 24/7 SERVICE
MOUNTAINS OF CUSTOMER DATA
... BURIED, UNUTILISED...
FINANCIAL INDUSTRY
As SOON as I have another VIABLE option, I'll be gone!
Yeah, don't think I'm STAYING BECAUSE I'm SATISFIED. I just can't be BOTHERED.
MOBILE OPERATOR
may be on the brink of being OVERTAKEN by other industries
You can't become a mobile operator but I CAN TURN INTO A PROVIDER of BANKING SERVICES!
SWINDLED ONCE, suspicious FOREVER
DON'T TAKE YOUR CUSTOMER FOR GRANTED
KNOWLEDGE CAPITAL & SOCIETAL IMPACT
will be measured alongside of MONETARY VALUE
are gaining in importance
TRUST ME.
must re-think how much they SELL (the best margin) instead of LOOK out for the CUSTOMER'S BEST INTERESTS
OUTSOURCING IS a PHASE
STEP ASIDE, DUDE!
EASY
CHEAP
FIRST WE OUTSOURCE TO SKILLED PEOPLE, THEN WE OUTSOURCE TO SKILLED MAC

FUTURE VISION
SERVICE
ADDING VALUE TO NUMBERS
KER of TRUSTWORTHY parties
CREDIT ASSESSMENTS of INDIVIDUALS & CO's
ION of MY BUSINESS
MY EXTERNALISED FINANCIAL ADVISOR
NAL service WITH PERSONALITY
ACTION
TO CATCH UP WITH
E REST
DATA to advice me?
VERY REMOTE & UN-INVOLVED!
Need FOR PROACTIVE ACTION
Why do I need to calculate my TRAVEL EXPENSES in EXCEL, when you have the information ALREADY!
STOP THEM?
HNOLOGICAL SHIFTS
OWER to the PEOPLE
Next generation of USERS see computers as a NATURAL TOOL
PEN SOURCE rises
MART SOFTWARE
a smart
nancial decision-
aker
I'm the GOOGLE of BANKING
DEATH of BANKING as we know it
Over 50% of transactions at London stock exchange are COMPUTER-MADE
go elsewhere
BUY!
DONATE TO CHARITY
MONEY
AGER
NOT THE BANK
Better keep my financial records myself
LINES OF CODE

# Peter Cochrane

Former CTO, British Telecom

As the former CTO of British Telecom, Peter Cochrane has a unique perspective on ICT and service institutions, such as banks. For Cochrane, banks are a building, a physical place where people go to for service. Traditionally, banks tend to be remote and detached, and "to operate as if they are some kind of industry, but actually they are a service." A typical customer wants to have the bank's support available to him/her anywhere in the world, at any time. Although electronic banking is available, the problem arises when the customer has special needs. Hence, the root of the problem lies with a bank's opening hours. As long as a customer needs more complex transactions that require greater interaction with a bank than through electronic banking, there will be a time delay. Voicemail and e-mail responses can be delayed, restricting people to specific times when they can actually phone the bank. With people constantly on the move worldwide, these restrictions are inconvenient at the very least.

Cochrane observes that banking today is rather static-passive. Banks have a lot of information about their customers and their lifestyles, yet do nothing with it. Instead of proactively offering financial advice and guidance, banks still wait for customer requests before reacting. He believes there needs to be a shift in attitude to a much more proactive approach in banking. This is not limited to financial advice, but also to security against credit card fraud. Oftentimes, large, one-off purchases by a credit card thief are caught by the company. However, smaller, regular purchases go unnoticed until the customer files a claim with the insurance company and begins a tedious, time-consuming process to get that money back. Cochrane thinks that financial services institutions could apply higher levels of vigilance to better serve their customers.

Cochrane finds ICT and security departments in banks devoid of purpose. Rather than dealing with knowledge management, providing more secure systems, and developing cutting-edge tracking systems, their main activity seems to involve supporting the last version of Microsoft Office or loading obscure applications on computers. He points out that the skills are there; more and more managers are very ICT-capable. If banks were to invest in changing their approach and leveraging the skills they already have in-house, then banking as a whole would change from being a remote, passive organisation to an active, ubiquitous p76 entity. Banking will happen everywhere and at any time. According to Cochrane, "It is going to be providing a service, and a lot of what it does is going to be based on the information of transaction of business that it has, and has so far failed to exploit." With the vast amount

*"Outsourcing is expedient because you can't find enough bodies; ultimately they will be replaced by machines."*

of information they have at their fingertips about their clients, banks are fully capable of assessing risks on behalf of their customers, but regrettably, ICT departments are not at that level of service and capacity yet.

If ICT departments were able to leverage the bank's knowledge, Cochrane believes that this knowledge could be used to provide better services for the customers, such as investment advice, security ratings, risk assessments and monitoring currency and political trends. Currently, customers must manage their own finances and conduct their own research. In the future, Cochrane believes that banks should become "all-pervasive."

He also finds a shortcoming in how banks process requests, suggesting that they are often very slow—no matter the type of request. Despite having good information on a customer's personal and financial information, banks remain relatively impersonal and there is no real relationship between the customer and the bank. A customer's account manager usually changes several times a year, giving account managers insufficient time to know the individual client. Cochrane describes the situation as "corporate memory loss." As banks continue to reduce their ranks, bank employees get more responsibilities, have less time to attend to customers, and personalized service declines further. Although the bank's intention is to maintain a high level of customer service, the process of reacquainting the customer with the new bank manager is time-consuming and inconvenient, especially in a fast-moving world.

Cochrane strongly believes that the financial services industry is ripe for a technological revolution. The history of financial services has seen the industry shift from bartering to the use of metal, to pieces of paper, to cheques, to cards and then credit. Cochrane suggests that the next transition will come in the form of the mobile phone and could emerge as a threat to the banking industry. Because mobile phones at the back end have a billing system, they can be used for payments, which could be invoiced on the monthly mobile phone bill or statement. He points out that "it is very difficult for a bank to become a mobile phone company, but it is very easy for a mobile phone company to become a bank." Small, quick transactions—buying a cup of coffee, buying a newspaper, renting a car—can be made with a mobile phone. Radio Frequency Identification (RFID) is also expected to play a major role in the near future. Cochrane predicts that RFID will have a great impact on the electronic point-of-sale and will have implications for insurance.

Suggesting another threat to financial services institutions, Cochrane speaks about the deteriorating loyalty of customers. Banks, which are unable to meet customer expectations, may lose them to the many alternatives that are increasingly available. If there are better deals, customers are more than likely to switch providers. In this, banks and telecoms share a similar risk. "The number one advantage that banks have is the same as the number one advantage of telecoms: the lethargy of the customer. They cannot be bothered to move, but if you upset them, they will leave, and you will not get them back." Cochrane warns banks to be particularly aware of this threat. Many financial services institutions will see profit margins shrink simply by spending inordinate amounts of money on acquiring new business and watching as customers move on for better deals. Banks must address the reality of people becoming increasingly self-sufficient and fully capable of looking after themselves. For Cochrane, the ideal business model for the bank is "for [the bank] to live in the customers' pocket to find out what their problems are and then come up with solutions to solve these problems." Banks can no longer afford to observe at a distance and be reactive. Being proactive will be key to a bank's success in connecting with the customer.

For Cochrane, the entry of new technology is a trigger for changes in the banking industry. Comparable to the transformation that occurred in the telecom industry when it was forced by the introduction of text messaging to invest in extra infrastructure—at the cost of making less money—banking will undergo an evolution. Not necessarily a bad development, this change could eliminate many of the inefficiencies and lack of service in the banking system, transferring them to a third-party service provider to perform at less cost to the customers.

To date, banking has been driven by money and Cochrane sees the world entering a new phase that is much more complex; one in which "[businesses] are going to have to account for not just the bottom line in dollar terms, but also in the way [the business] generates and manages knowledge." Knowledge capital will involve a social dimension that includes such
p76
considerations as carbon footprints.* Unfortunately, current accounting systems are solely money-based, suggesting a need for the complete reevaluation of the value placed upon people, the ecology, investments, and on society itself. Without true financial modeling, the system quickly becomes highly nonlinear and complex.

The convergence of the break-up of megasystems and cheaper memory creates an interesting situation where the individual is able to keep his/her own records. Rather than relegate

*"We could see the 'Google of banking': something which grows quickly, overnight almost, and becomes a dominant force."*

financial records to the banks, which rely upon mega computer systems, customers can rely on their own information to find individual records. Furthermore, Cochrane expects the individual to be more careful with this financial information than the bank.

In concluding his remarks, Cochrane briefly refers to a new technological paradigm whereby "computational power is going to be augmented by century capability". The world beyond Moore's Rule, he indicates, offers interesting alternatives and an entire frontier for p49 technological exploration.•

At some point we started to see the connections between the interviews, so that whole new worlds emerged. Writing the scenarios was a matter of shaping these worlds in language.

Pieter Ketting

# Victor d'Alfonso

**Senior Vice President of Financial Services, Patni**

Patni is an India-based company that "provides services of building systems, infrastructure management and business process outsourcing." Victor d'Alfonso views outsourcing as a way to lower the cost of delivering services to the end customer. Although there are other lower-cost providers in the world, he sees India as being one of the preeminent places for outsourcing due to the combined advantages of cost, education, the numbers of skilled players and cultural compatibility. Primarily English-speaking, India eases the transition and potentially lowers the perceived risk for businesses.

However, d'Alfonso emphasises that outsourcing is no longer just about cost. Increasingly, it is about building a business around a lower-cost environment and market leadership. Since cost differentials may eventually evaporate, companies must learn to reach some level of understanding about their business in order to perform smartly and effectively. He suggests that the knowledge or ability to work in the best possible way may not necessarily be housed only within the financial services institution. There are possibly other vendors who may do the job better—a reason that so many companies are outsourcing what they consider to be noncore components of their business.

On the development of technologies, d'Alfonso finds that there are no breakthroughs currently entering the market. The Internet was considered to be a breakthrough technology, but d'Alfonso does not see any new technologies that would have the same impact as the Internet has had on society and business. Instead, technology is poised to evolve. Leveraging the power of the Internet, financial services institutions will have to make decisions on the strategic future of their companies and how to deploy their workforce. According to d'Alfonso, there are no clear ideas of how an ICT department should support its business customer or the company's other departments within the financial institution—a situation that needs to be addressed urgently. Globalisation is driving companies to find better ways of collaboration—better collaboration techniques, better collaboration tools and better technology. While the Internet has secured our connectivity, the global nature of commerce is demanding a deeper level of collaboration.

D'Alfonso believes that financial services are generally driven by customer expectations. Since customers are becoming more demanding and smart and savvy about personal economic affairs, financial services institutions will be challenged to meet these demands without
p73 reducing profit margins.• Changing methodologies and approaches will require substantial

*"I had concerns and packed unnecessary things for my first trip to India; but, no more. I function within my limits now."*

thought, investment and proactive actions. D'Alfonso suggests that financial institutions recognise and accept the prospect of momentary failures without being deterred, and to learn to grow from those experiences.

For d'Alfonso, an ideal outsourcing relationship is one in which both parties sense a win-win situation, and both parties are turning a profit and maximising their profit margins. Trans-cultural relationships are difficult, and there will necessarily be some give-and-take from both sides. He points out that, "At the end of the day, it is all about the interplay of the real assets: the people at work." A successful outsourcing relationship is a perfect balance of innovation and hard skills, and is fundamentally based on trust.

Regarding ICT departments, d'Alfonso believes that in the near future, they will shift from managing technology change to organisational change management, which is how the organisation adopts and deploys technology. Since outsourcing is a deliberate and defined business strategy, managing this process is also part of the responsibilities of the bank's ICT department. Managing an outsourcing contract will require substantial communication and interaction between the parties. There must be a well-defined plan, but also flexibility in ideas, planning and execution. A deep understanding and trust between the parties will help ensure that flexibility yields benefits rather than obstacles for the relationship.

8.23 am: with 30 people interviewed for a total of 67 hours on three continents, we are ready to bring it to a strategic breakthrough in two long days...

# Jack van Driel

CTO, IBM Digital Media Benelux



As the CTO of IBM in Benelux, Jack van Driel has "worldwide responsibility for studying not only the impact of technology on society and organisations worldwide, but also on how technology can help society and organisations in realising benefits." His area of specialty is the interaction between society, organisation and technology. In hindsight, he recognises that some wrong decisions were made in how technology was implemented within ICT environments in financial institutions. He believes the problem lies not with the technology itself, but with the shift of these processes from manual to automated, making former processes obsolete. The entire industry now faces the challenge of implementing new products and services, and changing the way the customer is seen and heard.

Strategically, financial institutions need to make decisions based upon core competencies versus core business, as the core business of the bank is fairly straightforward. While these vary among banks, each financial services institution must identify and evaluate its competencies, and accept those that the bank is lacking. It would be better for the bank to outsource these areas to a qualified party who specialises in running these processes. However, van Driel warns that coordinating and managing the outsourcing process is never simple: "The actual value of whatever industry you are in is determined by how quickly you can assemble a service or a product for your specific client base, by orchestrating the processes of the goods from suppliers. In some cases, people do not even have their own processes, but they just orchestrate the process of bringing a service to a client or the development of a service to a client."

Van Driel observes that compliance is enforced by politicians who are elected by the people, who are at the end, customers of the institutions. However, compliance necessarily raises costs, and while people want to be customers of a company that is fair, honest and responsible, they are still reluctant to pay a premium for those goods and services. Ultimately, price will remain the primary driver over prevailing attitudes.

According to van Driel, the future role of ICT in financial services will be to create an experience for the client. This process is becoming more complicated than expected. There are more channels than before to reach the client. As things become more virtual and more electronic, banks should anticipate a future in which it will be extremely difficult to promote a brand through the Internet. One solution would be to integrate financial services into routine interfaces, such p59 as an electronic device, entertainment system, etc.• This is a challenging proposition since the

*"Real change comes from the outside; so, banking should look at others for creative solutions."*



brand would not come through the interface, whatever it may be. Therefore, as a channel, the Internet would be hidden behind the preferred interface.

Although people place a certain level of trust in their financial services providers, there is still very little personal contact between the customer and the bank. A trend will be for people to take more personal responsibility of their financial situation since the government will soon be unable to continue its support in this area. Van Driel believes that strong client interaction will become increasingly important. The bank needs to create specific solutions and products for specific clients, but the process must be accomplished efficiently. Van Driel suggests that this could be done with even 99% standard building blocks and 1% client-specific processes—a complicated proposal because it would require getting into all p57 the details of the company's business.

Van Driel sees lack of innovation in the financial services industry. He advises these institutions to look outside for real change, particularly at the electronics supply chain or the automotive industry. These industries have had their margins squeezed and are moving towards very creative solutions. He sees the financial services industry moving in the same direction and becoming more aware of these changes, but regrets that the industry is not moving quickly enough.

While it is generally understood that the role of ICT departments is to manage technology implementation and integration processes, the department's role is, in reality, much more complicated. Defining the processes and software components is a very important but difficult task for the management. For many institutions, this area has not been explored; thus, there is a lack of coherent definition about the business processes that are most important. Since discussions to prioritize business processes is difficult enough, van Driel warns against bringing technology into the discussion as it will create unnecessary complications. In his point of view, technology is not the root of the problem. Sooner or later, technological problems will be addressed—it is simply a matter of time. Today, the more straightforward processes can already be completely resolved by standard packages. For simple processes, it is highly likely a third party has designed the support; and the organisation only needs to tie this to its other processes. In an extreme situation, a financial services company could potentially function without any ICT people and without an ICT department. The institution only needs to design and assemble the processes, and then find a third party to run a standardised process.

Van Driel finds that most of the systems currently in use by financial institutions are very well engineered; but, they were also developed with a view that the bank has complete control over the environment. However, after these many years, the systems have become outdated and cumbersome. These so-called legacy systems will never be completely eliminated, but it is becoming increasingly clear to financial services institutions that it is no longer economically rational to continue investing in old technology.

Van Driel advocates the involvement of ICT people in bank processes since ICT staff understand architecture, system design and design principles. While he admits that these elements only apply to their environment—theoretical understanding about how things work—how to design a system involves not only technical knowledge but also understanding business process. Therefore, consulting its ICT department will enable the bank to design a new architecture and new business processes that can benefit the business end in the long run. Where banks uncover trouble is in interaction with the client, and finding ways to keep the customer happy. Technology is an important enabler of new business ideas and value creation, but technology sometimes fails because it simply has not yet matured. However, van Driel encourages financial services institutions to just "do it in the Japanese way—do not find the one responsible for the problem—just solve it."

iFLEX, CEO iFLEX Organizing

through the UNDERSTANDING of HUMAN
in DIFFERENT SITU

PHYSICAL

EMOTIONAL

FINANICAL

How will we manage CULTURAL DIFFERENCES?

How will PEOPLE act?

IT's always PEOPLE who use the TECHNOLOGY

MANAGING the INTERDEPENDENCY

FINANCIAL services, communications & TECHNOLOGY are interdependent

UNDERSTANDING the BEHAVIOURS

- What makes us human beings?
- How do we act and REact?

CONSTRAINTS FEED innovations, LIMITS FIRE up creativity

Use this INSIGHT into BASIC HUMAN MOTIVATIONS also in BUILDING your OUTSOURCING SYSTEM.

LASSI for 1000 customers COMING UP!


- Build SHARED SUCCESS with 50-50 partnership

COMMITMENT included!

GIMME BETTER
PRICE!
SQUEEEEZE out all you can!

Focus on SAVING or MAKING money?


BUYING the CHEAPEST or BUILDING the BEST?

Anuka

PUT your DATA to use!
Think PROACTIVE, then ACT
customer
OUCHPOINT produces
valuable INFORMATION
How can we use this data to BEST ADVANTAGE
n't CARE LESS about
egacy systems Just
the SERVICES SERVE ME!
Customer data as an ASSET
How good are we at INTEGRATING these two?
e BEST system
will not be good enough,
if you don't understand
the SOUL of your
customer
WHEREVER they are
INNOVATE &
INTEGRATE with SPEED
ed to MAKE UP
CONSTRAINED!
ECENOMIC IMBALANCE
GGEST RISK
India
managing the
SHIFT

# Deepak Ghaisas

CEO, India Operations, and CFO, iFlex Solutions Ltd.

Deepak Ghaisas has worked in the software industry since 1987. In his opinion, the world is going to be borderless. Instead of geographical boundaries to distinguish countries, the world will be differentiated by cultural differences. Even so, cultural distinctions are blurring as the world comes closer and closer together, encouraging greater transcultural collaboration, practices and behaviour. The blurring of differences, coupled with technological advances, will drive greater interdependence among financial services, communication and technology. The interdependency of these three elements will deliver market success. Ultimately, that success will depend on consumer behaviour, what their expectations are, and whether those expectations have been met.

Financial services institutions have an easily available wealth of information about their customers, which can be leveraged with information technology to great institutional advantage. Ghaisas believes that people give unnecessary importance to technology when talking about ICT; and suggests that more importance be given to the information part of the equation. “Technology is the enabler; it is an information arbitrage that will make you lead the industry. How you can best make use of the information that you have will give you competitive advantage.” According to Ghaisas, there may not even be a need for banks in 15 years. Banking will still be necessary, but banks themselves may not be required. With nonbanking financial companies competing more with banks than banks are doing with each other, customers have an infinite array of possibilities.

p58 Ghaisas sees three primary challenges for banks: innovation, integration and speed.° To accomplish this, part of the strategy lies in outsourcing noncore components. Ghaisas warns, however, that this is not enough. The best way would be to create a win-win situation in which the bank’s outsourcing partner and the people who are managing the outsourcing relationship also flourish. Failures are experienced together. Ghaisas believes that these experiences will help strengthen the relationship.

On the importance of flexibility for banks, Ghaisas explains that the financial industry must be the first to quickly respond to the economy's ups and downs. Faced with constraints, the banking sector must necessarily become more innovative to overcome obstacles—in technology, in regulations, in economic health etc. As an example, Ghaisas believes that the constraints of poverty have spurred India to become very innovative, and sees great potential for the country to grow exponentially in a very short time.

Christian Goeckenjan

# Christian Goeckenjan & Richard Lowrie

VP, Industry Solution Management; Director of Banking Strategy, SAP Financial Services

Starting with a rhetorical question about whether he will still have his position as an employee of a software company in 10 years, Goeckenjan contemplats a more centralised environment in which consolidation would become a trend for certain functions. One person could do a job or task that previously required many other employees to perform. Adding to this view, Lowrie wonders what the new jobs will entail and how ICT employees could prepare themselves for this new future.

Goeckenjan expects consolidation in the financial services industry, suggesting that there will be fewer, but much larger banks and financial institutions in five to 10 years. He believes also that there will no longer be entities that are clearly and simply financial services providers in the future, because they will start merging with other services, such as utilities, retail and others. This suggests that, although there will still be ICT professionals, they will probably not be within the ICT department of the bank. Most likely the bank will have "incorporated its own ICT department, made that a smaller company, and finally spun it off and made this company work for the provider," says Goeckenjan.

p75 p59

The role of ICT, according to Goeckenjan and Lowrie, is that of process control, rather than process management, at every stage of the value chain. To overcome problems associated with giving up elements that are not value creators while retaining control, financial organisations will need to look at their current position, consider where they think they will be headed in the future, and develop strategies or objectives towards these goals. However, there seems to be an "incredible lack" of internal assessment of what the core competencies are, Goeckenjan and Lowrie propose four core competencies of financial institutions:

- Customer relationship management;
- Understanding and managing or controlling risk;
- Complete management and control of the regulatory requirements; and
- Managing the brand.

Considering this initial list of core competencies, and recognising the many other tasks and services also performed by banks, one might spot many elements that should not be a core part of the bank's competencies. Different banks have different core competencies; and those that fall outside this consideration should be abandoned entirely or set up in such a way that the bank can still retain process control, but does not perform the entire service.

# *"When insurance companies ask for auditing systems for ICT risk management—that will create different ICT."*



Goeckenjan and Lowrie both expect new, disruptive forces, such as the Internet, to change the way the financial sector does business. Both see Google as potentially unsettling for financial services. Because it is easy to use and popular for finding information, customers can use Google to easily and quickly find the best financial service or the best place to get a mortgage. Another potentially disruptive trend is the drastic reduction in the number of skilled people in the ICT sector. As financial institutions lose more and more skilled programmers from their existing workforce, they will find it more costly to sustain the underlying expertise provided by the programmers to maintain business processes. A third potential disruption may be caused by new entrants to the sector. Most banks define their preferred customer segment by net worth and assets. However, a new breed of financial services is gradually emerging. These new providers service low-income consumers in emerging markets—BRIC countries and others, such as Mexico and South Africa.

According to Goeckenjan and Lowrie, financial institutions can develop much smarter ways of handling customer relationships as a bulwark against such disruptive developments. Banks currently do not manage relationships; they manage customer data. Despite collecting customer data, banks have been remarkably slow in taking that data and converting it intelligently to proactively manage those customer relationships. A monolithic internal ICT would most likely be unable to deliver this change, which would enable the emergence of agile, flexible environments. Aside from managing customer relationships, banks will also need to become better at managing competitor relationships. Goeckenjan and Lowrie expect that in the near future there will be a more complex relationship network in which people provide services in one area, compete in another, and cooperate in other areas with different support structures and organisations outside. There will no longer be a clear-cut competitor, friend, supplier or vendor. It is equally likely that a bank's fiercest competitors will also be its biggest collaborators. Therefore, entities that can build complex relationships will be successful more quickly.

Goeckenjan and Lowrie find that globalisation tends to balance out inequalities. They expect that at some point in the future, India may not be the preeminent labour market. Since it is impossible to predict where the next stable, sensible, meaningful labour market will be, companies need to develop strategies to hedge their bets.

"The current state-of-the-art technology is a legacy of tomorrow." For Goeckenjan and Lowrie, the reasons for the current legacy systems are manifold. The financial sector works faster and earlier to adopt ICT than do other industries. Banks are also highly dependent on ICT: if the system is down, the bank is down. Furthermore, the mindset of the financial sector is to stay fully in control of the bank's processes and its future. This means that the banking sector has built its ICT infrastructure layer upon layer, resulting in a highly complex system—so complex, in fact, that more often than not, financial services institutions leave these legacy systems alone rather than try to replace them. However, the convergence of new, more flexible entrants to the sector, industry consolidation and regulations might act as a trigger for banks to address their legacy systems in order to remain competitive.

p57
Sharing his views on software packages and outsourcing, Goeckenjan remarks that software packages are inevitable. Even so, financial institutions must realise that, although software packages are most likely to present fewer difficulties in the form of bugs and errors, the real problem will be to manage the integration of the packages into a single interface. Therefore, the organisation will need to first think about the architecture and system landscape before centralising and decentralising the processes, and then determine where and how the package is to be used. As for outsourcing efficiency, Geockenjan does not believe that it will be achieved by handing a problem area to someone else. For Goeckenjan, "effectively outsourcing means that you have to become better in defining the true process that you want to manage. Only after that can you give it to someone [else]."

Discussions at dinner after a day of hard work would involve a slightly broader view on the future. Some of us found inspiration here to start a new political party: Green-Right.

# Ashwin Goyal

VP and General Manager, Siebel Financial Services

At the time of the interview, Siebel was about to merge with Oracle. As a senior manager of Siebel Financial Services, a primary provider of software packages to Rabobank, Ashwin Goyal shares his expertise in observations about the direction of ICT in financial services and the impacts of ICT solutions, such as software packages and outsourcing.

In Goyal's view, Siebel's job is "to understand how banks use [Siebel's] software to better manage their customer relationships." He believes that 80% of what a bank does is strikingly similar to the operations performed by other banks. The remaining 20% of the bank's work differentiates it from the others. Siebel's objective is to build and deliver solutions to address the 80%, which would also give the bank the tools and the ability to extend coverage to the remaining 20% of the work. The trend towards standardisation is driving banks to separate their business processes based on the 80%-20% ratio. In doing so, banks are orienting themselves increasingly towards better understanding of their customers. To Goyal, this heightened appreciation allows banks to generate a comprehensive list of products that are designed to help customers meet their financial needs. Depending on a customer's stage in life, the needs may be particular. However, financial services providers must be aware that this involves more than simply offering the right set of products. Goyal believes it calls for a holistic approach to creating customer experience so that the customer recognises the bank as meeting his/her financial needs, that it provides the right set of products, and that it anticipates where the customer is going with his/her needs and preferences. A financial services institution that is able to create this level of experience for every customer will forge a much stronger bond with its clientele. This is particularly important in the current context where individual customers often manage multiple financial relations: checking account, savings account, mortgages, insurance policies, etc. A deeper relationship has the potential to influence a customer's decision about whether to maintain all their financial relationships or to consolidate them into fewer numbers of service providers. If they are moved to consolidate, it is most likely that the preferred service providers will be the ones having a strong presence in the customer's life.

Goyal sees the competitive landscape changing rapidly. Nontraditional service providers, such as Wal-Mart, are entering the financial sector. Smaller banks are forced to contend with megabanks that offer a "one-stop-shop" model. Goyal suggests that banks ask themselves how a bank can be more agile in responding to customer needs. To Goyal, bundled products are one possibility. However, they should not be a one-size-fits-all bundle. Instead, banks and

*"We are about increasing value, increasing complexity. It should be about increasing value, decreasing complexity."*

their ICT departments must be able to make personalized offerings based on their knowledge of customer needs. In order to do this, banks must shift from being transaction-oriented to becoming more relationship-oriented. Goyal observes that technologies are now available to better enable banks to accomplish this.

Goyal predicts that banks will have to specialise over the course of the next decade. Although some will head towards a megabank model, others will divest business lines that are not relevant to their core business and specialise in those areas where they believe they have a competitive advantage. Still, other banks may explore the potential for cross-selling with p74 nonfinancial partners, such as retail centres. An important question is whether the intermediary channel is part of the bank's strategy to "white-label" the bank's products and services, or whether a direct customer relationship is more in line with the bank's culture and business model. Although the basic principle of keeping customers happy is still valid, there are many uncertainties to maintaining a direct customer relationship. The banks can adapt to meet emerging customer needs if they understand how customer behaviour is changing and how to respond to the changes.

Goyal believes that outsourcing is a major trend and not a passing phase. He cites economic consideration—getting the job done at less cost—as the reason. Although outsourcing is an attractive option on the surface, quality is a fundamental concern. While he supports the practice, Goyal cautions financial institutions to outsource in a smart way: by understanding it thoroughly before investing in it. Starting with the first step of developing a list of important criteria, companies should outsource business processes gradually, allotting time for adjustments. In the face of trends to standardise and outsource, Goyal believes that ICT departments in financial services institutions will shift their focus from building and maintaining all of the bank's applications to concentrate on the 20% differentiator.

Goyal suggests that as the business environment becomes increasingly complex, so will the ICT environment. This complexity will add more cost. At some point, the value proposition of adopting new technology will become less interesting; and Goyal sees the pace of innovation p66 and ICT adoption eventually slowing down. As technology is adopted less and less often, innovation will decline. Small service-oriented businesses may emerge to offer services to manage this complexity; but, in many cases, it will simply replace one kind of complexity with another, starting the same cycle again. Because there is little monetary value to solving the problem,

Goyal believes that the issue of complexity has not really been addressed. He predicts, however, that it will eventually be more valuable to find a solution to the complexity problem than to resolve the problem of product innovation.

Regarding open source, Goyal believes it will be the next wave for ICT development because of its proven viability. He expects open source to be widely adopted, and suggests that fighting against it would be detrimental to the business in the long run. Financial institutions need to promptly develop a model that will enable the organisation to seamlessly coexist with open source in a way that ultimately adds more value to [the] customers.

It sounds surreal: a group of ICT managers modeling their strategic future in clay, in four different works of art. I wouldn't have believed you before if you told me that I was going to throw a fully prepared presentation for the next day in the bin, doing the whole thing in clay instead.

Pieter Ketting

# Eric van Heck

Professor ICT Management, RSM Erasmus University

An authority on ICT in the business context, Professor van Heck's field of expertise is the interface between business and information technology.

Van Heck expects increasing complexity in financial products and services in the next five to ten years in such areas as payments, settlements, risks, mortgages, insurance, etc. The uncertainty surrounding the issue relates to the magnitude of the increase in complexity and how it is managed. To van Heck, the companies that can manage the complexities successfully will be the winners in the long run. This will drive financial institutions to modularise and personalise their services and products.

Although technology can be used successfully to improve relationships between people, it can also set relationships back when too much technology replaces human interaction. Ultimately, people are social animals, and constant interaction with computers may not be as appealing as expected. If banks were to move away from the traditional top-down business model towards a more collaborative approach, they would most likely experience a different wave of innovation. Van Heck recognises, however, that different cultural subgroups have different ideas and needs. "As a financial institution, [the bank] has to think about how [it] can target these different groups in such a way that they feel that they have their personalised products, while in the back office, the bank modularises in such a way that [it] will create a kind of mass p74 customisation approach."*

The financial services sector in Europe is still a level playing field, where each financial institution has its own piece of the pie. However, with more entrants into the market, van Heck expects that higher levels of competition will change this situation. The long-term stability enjoyed by local banks will quickly become unbalanced. To survive, van Heck believes that financial services institutions should be more careful about adopting CRM systems. He advocates examining the human interaction between a bank employee and the bank's customers before considering how ICT may be leveraged to improve that relationship. He does not agree that placing CRM systems at the centre of the business model is a way of placing customers at the centre as well. In his opinion, when the architecture is too CRM-centric the customer is often too easily forgotten. He warns against adjusting the organisation to the system: it would eliminate the company's competitive advantage as it would almost be the same system as its competitors'. By contrast, when the system

*"The customer interface must be very simple, and inside, enormously complex; the challenge is to balance the two."*

is adjusted to the organisation, then it continues to retain those elements that give the organisation its competitive edge—a much more sustainable business model in the longer term.

For the future, van Heck envisions a business world that will demand some basic, critical business capabilities, such as the ability to manage the network of companies around the organisation; to manage the customer and the network of customers; to manage sourcing relationships; and to manage very complex products. If these critical abilities are not present within the financial sector, we can expect to see the emergence of nontraditional providers that possess these capabilities and are willing and capable of meeting changing customer needs.

The business side of an organisation and its ICT department constantly struggle to understand each other. Neither side fully understands the role of the other, resulting in a complicated situation. There is no true solution to the problem, but van Heck describes some models that are currently in use by companies to resolve the issue. The first is a partnership model in which the ICT department is seen as the innovative partner for the business side. The second model uses ICT as a platform, whereby a platform is built for business, such as eBay. The third is a scalable model in which ICT is given resources, infrastructure, software and hardware to quickly scale up or down to accommodate the business operations. Depending on the bank's business model, any of the three approaches can work.

Van Heck offered the following advice for change in the financial services sector:

- Change the organisation's approach from one centered on the individual organisation to a networked approach;
- Change from an individual customer focus to a networked customer focus in which the bank learns how customers network and form alliances, and finds ways to leverage this;
- Change from a functional role, with all the legacy systems into a system that is more CRM-oriented; and
- Change from traditional insourcing to different kinds of sourcing, both outsourcing and insourcing.

RABOBANK
Theo Huibers
DIR, KPMG Business Advisor Services
PROF. on Computer Science, University of Twente
CREATE
ALIGNMEN
I've been here for EVER and I'm gonna stay here
FOREVER.
BIG PLAYA
THAT'S where you're WRONG!
FAST 1
ICT & INTERNET-enabled WORLD
FREEDOM of CHOICE
for consumers
CHANGE of ATTITUDE
for COMPANIES
I PICK and MIX
What's your WISH?
the BEST for me!
DEVELOPING SYSTEMS
emotion recognition
avatars as guides
rules of engagement:
INTERACTION
CO-OPERATION
COMMUNITY CREATION
New look at the ROLE of BANK
DEFINE core competen
DEFINE position in VALUE CHAIN
MANAGE CHANGE carefully
FOCUS is crucial
Who'll be the GOOGLE of BANKING?
TRUST
How do you LEVE
the STRENGTHS
Huh! How CLOSE or FAR is this to our CURRENT COMPETENCES?
SNIP!
INNOVATION REQUIRED!
What's the NEXT BIG THING?
The NEXT BIG thing can't be predicted
IT CAN ONLY be CREATED
CREATED, perhaps, but NEVER GUARANTEED.
Can we OUTSOURCE innovation?
What's the FOCUS?

Let's outsource to get SAVINGS!
BUSINESS
ICT
LONG-TERM
VISION
Jaa...! suppose it's India
or nothing...
or maybe China...
Risks of
• INSTABILITY
• RISING COSTS
COST-CONSCIOUS FUTURE PERSPECTIVE
ADOPT the BUSINESS PERSPECTIVE
It's not a GIVEN "HAPPILY EVER AFTER"
Can we get a better RETURN on the money saved in
outsourcing by INVESTING IT ELSEWHERE?
HOW MUCH
• TECHNOLOGY
• INFORMATION
• ATTENTION
IS ENOUGH?
I don't want to spend more time on my finances
than I MUST. Take care of it for me!
Is there enough
TRUST?
RELIABILITY
EXPECTATIONS

# Theo Huibers

Director, KPMG Business Advisor Services, and Professor, Computer Science, University of Twente

As a computer science professor at the University of Twente, Theo Huibers has long followed the way value chains are changing, due to ICT, for many different areas, including information, Internet behaviour and the world of Google. He is particularly interested in the impact of ICT on media, education and organisations, such as financial institutions. During his many years in the technology sector, Huibers has seen how the Internet or ICT brings power to the customer. Before the power of the Internet, companies developed products and services which were then pushed on customers. Since the rise of the Internet, customers have greater freedom to pick and choose, such as buying music by individual song rather than by the entire album.

According to Huibers, the world is changing rapidly and by 2017, many of the big names in business today may no longer exist, or may change into some other entity. Huibers questions which ones will turn out to be mammoths that die out, and which ones will adapt and remain. As organisations, Huibers believes that banks run the risk of becoming mammoths because of the very nature of financial services. He encourages financial services institutions to change their role, becoming, perhaps, financial information aggregators or even directors of the entire financial process. Not every bank possesses the same core competencies, nor is it possible to be best-in-class in each area of the value chain. For Huibers, therein lies the dilemma of being a one-stop-shop for financial services. Megabanks, which bring all services under one roof, will be under pressure to be very good in all areas. However, due to the Internet and ICT, it is no longer necessary to have all the products and services housed in one firm because the customer can easily access different services, as long as the chain is managed correctly. The problem is in managing the chain successfully.

Huibers also shares insights from his long experience in the field of emotion management, putting a human face on the user interface by exploring human-media interaction rather than only computer-text interaction. He believes that new technology for the front office may p59 come in the form of an avatar or some other form.* The purpose will be to enhance human-media interaction.

Because of the increasing complexity of the business world, focus is a necessity. If the bank's strategy is to emphasise the importance of the customer and interaction, then the bank must focus on all the things happening in that area, such as human-media interaction. If the bank chooses to focus on competence, then it needs to target operational excellence. Figuring out the focus is perhaps the most difficult decision to make. For the financial sector, a basic

*"Cut costs for short-term interests; innovate for long-term profits."*



focus area is, perhaps, trust. Credit ratings and public reputation all contribute to the level of trust that the bank establishes between the institution and its clients. Specifically regarding Rabobank, Huibers believes it is known as a very trustworthy company with a strong relationship with its customers. As a possibility, Huiber proposes that Rabobank become a universal service provider of client contacts and knowledge, a potentially viable undertaking since everything is about collaboratively working on the Internet. While this would be on the front end, the back office could then be operated by another firm.

For Huibers, it is uncertain whether the value proposition, currently offered by outsourcing, will remain so. However, it is certain that the more business processes are split, the more the organisation will experience management and coordination problems. As a change, financial services institutions should consider insourcing. They should identify the areas the company is best in and determine whether the necessary skills and capabilities exist yet within the organisation. Huibers also emphasises that outsourcing be done for the right reasons.
He cautions that in outsourcing ICT, focusing on cost may create problems in the future because of innovations down the line. However, if the focus is on outsourcing operational excellence with the ICT company as a partner in innovation, then this may solve the innovation problem. Information and information technology change too rapidly for an organisation to depend on information storage or data connections. A financial services institution that relies too heavily on information storage or data connections runs the risk of becoming a
p49 mammoth in a very short time.*

Huibers foresees a shortage of skilled ICT people in the next decade. Managing ICT in this context will be a challenge for financial services institutions worldwide. They will need to focus on aligning ICT with business, human-media interaction and changing consumer markets. Instead of selling a digital dream and gadgets, the organisation will move towards the management of the information society and keeping clients. As for innovation, the challenge will lie with spotting new issues and concepts, new service centres and front-back offices, and aligning all of these. He expects these changes to occur within the next five to 10 years.

# Brewster Kahle

**Director of the Internet Archive**





Brewster Kahle believes that companies have an optimum opportunity to radically rethink how ICT functions are performed, and he repeatedly emphasises the central importance of data in ICT systems. Pointing to developments in the field, he speaks about leveraging programming needs to seize the opportunity for a comprehensive analysis. Computers have dropped in price and storage is free; only programming remains expensive. Determining how to minimize programming needs opens the way for a radical review of ICT functions. He finds evidence of this happening among new companies. Unlike older peers that retrofit existing systems, new companies have thought it through and are thus able to run cheaper, p73 p48 more efficient ICT systems. He notes that the ICT budgets of banks "are enormous"; and that the assorted plans and attempts to reintegrate systems, following a corporate merger, are extremely inefficient. According to Kahle, "...the investments and style of the ICT groups that were built up make it so it's very difficult to merge practically." Among the hurdles that companies encounter are personnel issues and complicated systems that "nobody understands" and "everybody's afraid of." To Kahle, this is the moment to do something radically different and simple. Implying that the underlying data of a bank—transactions—are limited and manageable in volume, despite the "customs built up," he says, "I don't quite understand why a bank isn't a Microsoft NT box sitting in a closet and a bunch of human relations people dealing with customers."

He sees efficiencies in building software from scratch. He proposes that, like hardware, it should be designed for obsolescence and be thrown out every three to five years. Hardware wears out, and is periodically replaced by a new generation. In contrast, software continues to retain core pieces of earlier generations, and is built up into complicated, intimidating systems.

Kahle is emphatic about data. He points out that data is the valuable component to be saved from old systems, and strongly recommends that it be kept separate from the software. Critical of the trend to weave software into databases, Kahle is convinced that "it's got to be a disaster." He views financial contracts and transactions to be "respresentable relatively simply" and in "a program-independent" way. Programs can change with new technologies, and even with new hires in technical personnel who can bring the latest programming knowledge to bear. He says, "It's probably really hard to find a college graduate that says, 'I want a career in COBOL.'"

# *"ICT has become too complicated. We need to separate data from processes, and manage them differently."*



Expanding on the importance of data, Kahle says "files are key. The programmes? Who cares!" Still, he notes that this view changed with the advent of the personal computer—a change apparent in the differences between Unix and Microsoft Word files. "You wrote a Microsoft Word file," he says, "but it was sort of in some binary representation that all it cared about was being able to read it back into the programme". By comparison, Unix retains a focus on data by writing programmes that are easily manageable, understood and open to incremental—rather than system-wide—upgrades.

Kahle also speaks of changes taking place in programming language. As hardware and computing became inexpensive, work became increasingly computerised. This led to new developments in computer language or to "higher-level languages." According to Kahle, higher-level languages eliminate the need for purely technical hires: "people that are different from the people that communicate with people," implying a firm's freedom to bring in personnel who can better bridge the current digital divide between business and ICT staff. Additionally, new programming languages can make it possible for people doing user interfaces to be programmers themselves, allowing for more efficiencies.

Kahle finds that building and maintaining a database is costly, and advocates doing away with them entirely. Having tried and succeeded to some extent, he admits that it is difficult to operate completely without databases.

p75 He is hopeful about developments in visualising queries.• He spoke of more complicated, people-interactive interfaces that could help users with only limited training understand how to make queries or interact with systems. Referring to Amazon's order payment system as a successful example, he notes that the system's simplicity belies the many years of work required by this; including experimental runs—which Amazon conducted for its system, with larger and larger groups of users.

As with his emphasis on data, Kahle strongly advocates scaling down systems and using flat files. He observes that flat data is easy to write, and that in general tools should be kept small, understandable and dispensable. They should be easily built by small teams, implemented quickly, used and thrown away. Illustrating the value of scaled-down systems, Kahle recalls his work for Amazon, which reduced its annual ICT costs to 10% of the then-current transaction budget, and resulted in cost savings of $100 million. Having persuaded its top executive,

Jeff Bezos, to "stop buying hardware. Just stop!" Kahle's company took a strategic approach, analysing what worked and what didn't, and then rebuilding the system piecemeal using its knowledge of thought files and clusters of computers. "One of our big victories," says Kahle, "was helping them renegotiate their Internet contracts because they were paying more than they needed to."

Being in a scenario process is truly learning a new language. Where in the workshops we understood each other perfectly, using the same words to explain to others what we were doing sounded like Chinese to them; it really involved a translation to give them some idea of how we progressed.

Wil Leeuwis

# Heikki Karjaluoto

Professor, Faculty of Economics and Business Administration, University of Oulu



Published author and authority on the business of banking and e-commerce, Heikki Karjaluoto talks about the various reasons why people change financial services providers. People tend to switch providers when they take their first mortgage. Other than that first major change, most consumers are quite passive and remain with the same bank. Therefore, on that significant occasion in a consumer's life—when he/she is getting the first mortgage—it becomes important for banks to stay alert and make the best offer in order to win new business.

Karjaluoto believes that financial institutions have not been as active as other online players in improving the efficiency of their marketing. Unlike many other online companies, financial services institutions have failed to leverage online capabilities to "gather customer-oriented information, such as their buying habits, including the products and the quantity, online surfing habits, their online personalisation, and newsletter personalisation preferences" so that the website can be customized according to their preferences. Location marketing is covered as part of a possible future. This may help e-business, but security is an ethical issue. Not very many consumers will be comfortable with disclosing the location from where they are using their mobile phone. Although it is admittedly an effective strategy if the consumer is in the right place at the right time with the right message, it is still going to take some time for acceptance.

Through his studies, Karjaluoto has discovered that people want to have more personalised,
p67 human services from banks. Banking has become too faceless and impersonal. Although this
works on some level with most people, it does not contribute to bolstering consumer trust
p67 and loyalty. In creating a more humane and interactive atmosphere for customers, financial
services institutions may improve the brand value of the bank.

# Jongwan Kim

General Manager, Research, Woori Bank

Jongwan Kim works for the second largest bank in Korea, Woori Bank. He is responsible for studying the best way to use a digital banking strategy in the future. In Kim's opinion, the biggest uncertainties in the future are the kinds of technologies that will be developed; whether or not customers need a new digital banking service; and whether the new technology will have high acceptability among the customers. Kim also notes that there is a fundamental uncertainty about how digital banking contributes to a financial institution because of the difficulty inherent in quantifying ROI in digital banking investments.

Kim believes that technology can advance to the point where banking channels will multiply, and both digital banking (i.e., cyberbranch or channel) and offline channels will be available to banking customers. Such advanced technology will be accessible "without any 'log in' or time-wasting devices, where they have to connect to a website through their mobile phones or any other wireless devices." He predicts that developments in technology will increase the number of outlets for banking services in an innovative way. The most convenient channel will be the preferred channel for customers. Banks will also be able to introduce mobile banking services and products based on these new channel technologies. In the future, the increase in banking outlets will enable banking services to be accessed p76 anywhere at any time, greatly increasing the convenience of customers. "Ultimately, customers will be using banking services unconsciously because banking services will be absorbed in the customers' [daily] digital life." Kim finds that the current difficulty in developing digital banking service lies in the continuing lack of integrated technology services platform. Korea is at the forefront of the most progressive digital banking technologies. Even so, the ultimate goal is still to provide an integrated platform in which customers can access banking services any time. Compared to Korea, European banks still have a long way to go.

Kim believes that customers will demand personalised and customised services. Banks in turn will vie for the opportunity to satisfy those needs. He expresses his thoughts on attracting customers. Customers are driven by convenience, and face-to-face services between financial institutions and customers are becoming more about nonofficial transactions. Security will be another important element to consider: the more secure a customer feels, the more trust he/she will have in the financial services provider. He advises financial services institutions to consider the range of essential prerequisites for successful digital banking; such as, "online security, diverse and convenient channels and personal and

*"Make e-banking ubiquitous banking— with an integrated financial platform in all channels to access banking services any time."*

integrated financial information." He has observed changing customer needs, and is an advocate for customer-centred service. A thorough analysis of the customer's needs and timely provision of the service are, for Kim, perhaps the most decisive factors in the success of digital banking.

digital banking | mobile banking | ubiquitous banking | customer focus | convenience | Kim

RABOBANK
VIVEK KULKARNI
B2K Corp/ CEO & CHAIRMAN
SUCCESSFUL STRATEGIES for INDIA
KNOW THY
But if they're so smart, how do we keep them from STEALING our KNOW-HOW?
PARTNER in BUSINESS CRITICAL AREAS
with great care
STOP! THIEF!
THE THING that makes us UNIQUE
Asking the Oracle
WHAT
FINANC
SERVIC
the FU
Plan for management HAND-OVER
We want to KEEP CONTROL
Treat TALENT with RESPECT, give interesting WORK
BANK
SHOP
Anyone can give FINANCING, sell INSURANCE & manage INVESTMENTS
Give the BEST JOBS to the BEST PEOPLE
Jolly good work, old chap!
GIVE UP on the IMPERIALISTIC attitude
MY BANK is open RIGHT NOW, RIGHT HERE
What will the MARKET look like?
I can RE-CONN you with your CUSTOME
THE WINNER is the one who captures the HEART of the CONSUMER
With room to grow and DEVELOP, too!
INVEST in creating UNDERSTANDING
This is it!
You mean ?
Allow for ITERATION to reach SHARED VISION
Bangalore says
This is the NEXT 6-8 year challenge for us in India!
GROWING SKILLS BEYOND engineering

KNOW WHAT YOU DO WELL!
SIMPLICITY, Please!
Uh...collect information about our customers...
YOUR CUSTOMER
How will BANKS keep in TOUCH WITH THE CUSTOMER?
Customers come to us because we keep their money safe
VIP
WHERE'S THE SERVICE?
HOW LONG WILL IT BE ENOUGH?
Managing MILLIONS of MICRO LOANS
The LINE between PRODUCT & SERVICE is DISSOLVING
We welcome the WORLD!
PENNESS
feeds success in the GLOBAL ECONOMY
uires even more SOLID
RASTRUCTURE
which we don't
uite have YET!

# Vivek Kulkarni

CEO and Chairman, B2K Corp.

As a former ICT Secretary of the state of Karnataka in India, Vivek Kulkarni was one of the preeminent figures in the emergence of Bangalore as a leading centre for ICT worldwide. His mandate was to create an environment to attract technology and ICT companies. Partly through his efforts, Bangalore, like Silicon Valley, has become a name synonymous with the ICT sector.

In Kulkarni's opinion, almost every company may be considered successful in terms of ICT development. The only difficulty he sees is among companies that hold on to their own managers, deploying them to foreign countries, rather than rely on local management. If companies outsource to countries like India, then they must place a certain level of trust in the skills and capabilities of the outsourcing country. Kulkarni believes that, comparatively speaking, there is sufficient talent in India; however, because of tremendous growth and the inflow of many companies into India, the employment landscape may change within the next five to 10 years. Since the demand for skilled employees is high, and people may leave jobs that are not interesting or workplaces that lack close ties between employees and management, companies may run into an attrition problem. The trick is to properly manage the talent that is available in the organisation and to hire talent that fits the job. "The talent is available here right now. Because of this availability, you have a choice, and therefore you are able to get a better workforce."

Kulkarni sees outsourcing as a complicated process that, if done incorrectly, has a high chance of failure. He believes that a lot of time and effort must be invested in setting up an outsourcing centre. People from both parties should interact with each other frequently, even going to the point of making cultural visits to better understand the project and project requirements. Kulkarni finds that the rush of foreign firms into the Indian market has triggered increased labour costs. Although it is uncertain whether growth will continue for skilled labour, it cannot be denied that India has experienced a "percolation of culture" that is changing the characteristics of the next generation of workers. Younger generations of Indians are adopting American and European ways, diverging from the more frugal attitudes of their Indian elders. This different culture will likely yield a different set of skills. The question remains how the skills will be absorbed into the workforce in the next six to eight years.

Kulkarni draws a distinction between participative outsourcing and contracting. Participative outsourcing, or a partnership approach, should be considered in the context of "very critical

# *"Just 25% of Bangalore produces as many engineers as all of Ireland."*

technologies which [are needed] to maintain a good workforce." The greatest challenge in this is keeping people motivated and productive for the company. While partners do not work for competitors, contractors, however, are free agents, hired to simply deliver a product or a service, and are free to work for anyone else. In the future, Kulkarni predicts that financial services will change. Currently, people place their money in the bank primarily for safety reasons, with some guarantee that that money will still be there tomorrow. However, more and more nontraditional providers are emerging in the market and will most likely continue to—
p48 p73 until almost anyone can be perceived as a bank. A telecom company can effectively be a bank. A university can be a bank in offering an education loan, and advice on repayment options upon graduation. To Kulkarni, the possibilities are endless. He warns that unless banks find a new angle of approach, they will be unable to maintain their current position, which is largely based upon the client-bank relationship. Kulkarni strongly believes that customer information is key. "The person who keeps in touch with the consumer will win; everyone else will become a commodity." Although Kulkarni observes that banks are losing touch with their customers, he is optimistic that ICT is the answer, and that it can help the bank and its customers remain in touch.

Kulkarni suggests that a financial institution's long-term strategy should determine whether it should go to India and Bangalore. If the bank decides to become a global brand, then it will need to "understand different cultures [because of the introduction of] different products to different countries and financial systems." India is where the bank should go for technical manpower; ideally, adopting a partnership model. Bangalore is an attractive option for many companies because of its multicultural strength. English is the common language since only 30% of Bangalore's population speak the local tongue, Kannada, and the other 70% speak other languages. Thus, English is the international language of business and the city's common tongue by default. Kulkarni believes that as long as foreigners continue to come to Bangalore, the city will grow as it welcomes anyone with talent.

To Kulkarni, the line between service and product is increasingly blurred. "Without good service, the product is meaningless." The best product in the world will not be able to retain a loyal following if the supporting service is poor. The idea of service includes knowing what the customer needs and being able to provide a product that exactly fits the customer's
p74 requirements. As a personal example, Kulkarni notes that he uses only about 5% of Microsoft Excel features, but pays 100% of the price. By the time he learns a few more features, a new

version is out, and he must update his version again. This makes using Microsoft products particularly frustrating. By contrast, the music industry was transformed by iTunes, which allowed customers to listen to just one or two songs rather than oblige them to buy an entire album. The customer could now make purchases by the song—one of the key factors of iTunes' success.

To Kulkarni, service is a deciding factor in the success of a company's business model. Information is becoming ubiquitous, and everyone can access the same information. Therefore, the competitive advantage derived from customer information is disappearing, and what remains will be "the personalised services and relationships, which cannot be outsourced."

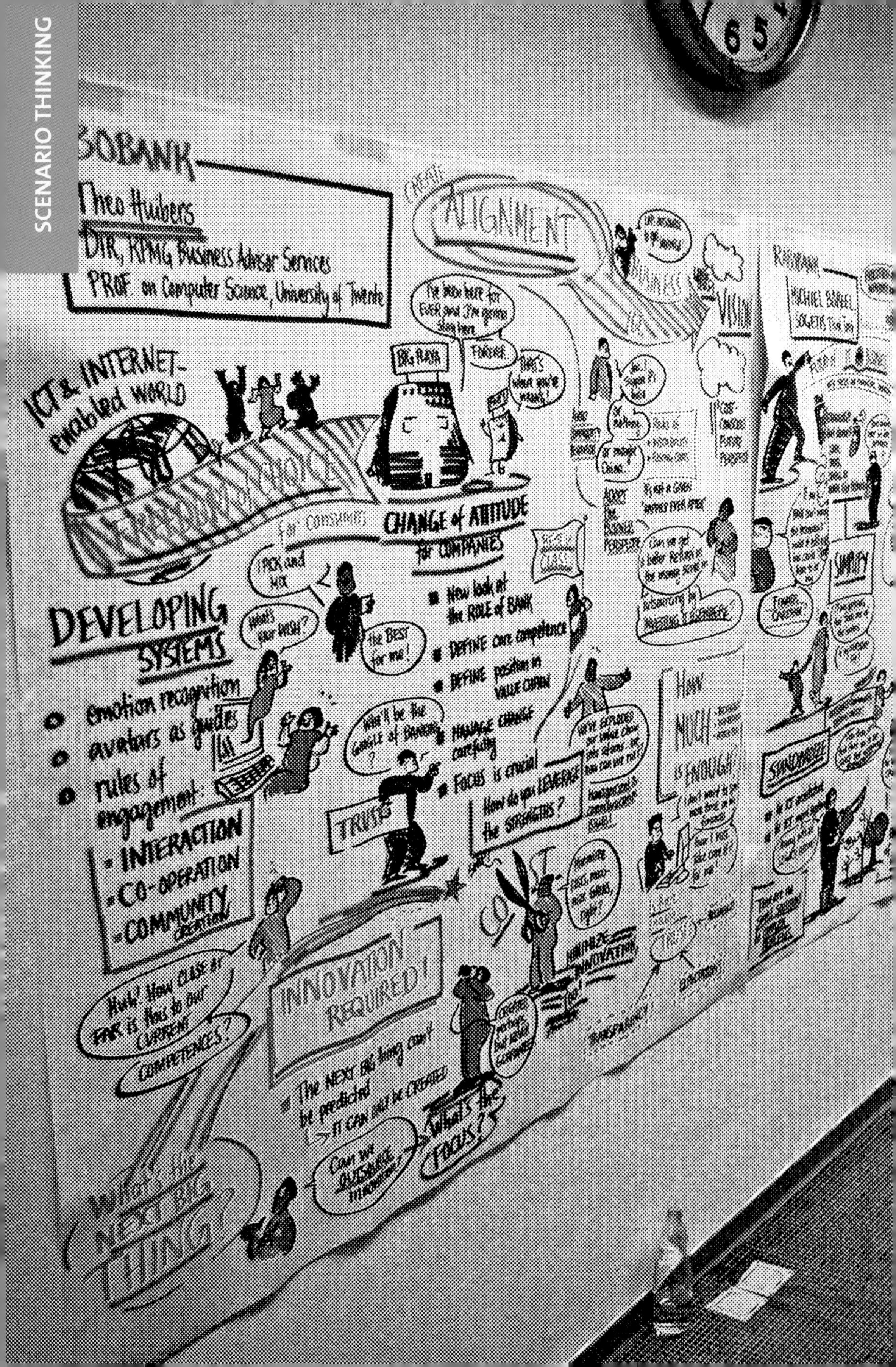

BOBANK
Theo Huibers
DIR, KPMG Business Advisor Services
PROF. on Computer Science, University of Twente
ALIGNMENT
ICT & INTERNET-enabled WORLD
CHANGE of ATTITUDE for COMPANIES
■ New look at the ROLE of BANK
■ DEFINE core competence
■ DEFINE position in VALUE CHAIN
■ MANAGE CHANGE carefully
■ FOCUS is crucial
How do you LEVERAGE the STRENGTHS?
DEVELOPING SYSTEMS
• emotion recognition
• avatars as guides
• rules of engagement:
= INTERACTION
= CO-OPERATION
= COMMUNITY CREATION
I PICK and MIX
What's your WISH?
The Best for me!
Who'll be the GOOGLE of BANKING?
TRUST
INNOVATION REQUIRED!
■ The NEXT BIG thing can't be predicted
→ IT CAN ONLY BE CREATED
Can we MEASURE INNOVATION?
What's the FOCUS?
What's the NEXT BIG THING?
HOW MUCH IS ENOUGH
COST
VISION
SIMPLIFY

The beautiful visualisation of interviews and scenarios made the core of the stories visible, which worked very well in the discussions that we had standing around the visualisations. That also makes it easy to remember the core of the interviews and scenarios.

Jeanne Driessen

# Praveen Kumar

Head of Financial Services Practice, Infosys U.K.

As the head of the Financial Services Practice for Infosys, Praveen Kumar works with large institutions in the financial services industry, looking into the key issues that the institutions are trying to address. In his opinion, if the organisation has a strong business model and a value proposition, then location is practically irrelevant. Recognising that globalisation has had an impact on the role of ICT in banking, Kumar speaks of two focal areas for banks from an ICT perspective. The first concerns the cost of doing incremental business. This business model works when the organisation is able to service higher and higher volumes at a lower incremental cost. ICT's role here, from an operational perspective, is to build the underlying platforms that enable growth, transaction processing and risk control. The second focal area is the need to build "a global capability from an internal service delivery perspective." Financial services need to build shared services and consolidate functions wherever possible, allocating that shared service model in the right geographical area. ICT's role in this case is to reconfigure the business to become more modularised to allow for agility and flexibility, giving the organisation the "leading edge of sustainable competitive advantage."

Kumar understands that from a CIO's perspective, it is of utmost importance to do more for
p58 p66 less.* This requires a different way of thinking, looking at opportunities to eliminate costs. Offshoring and outsourcing have been touted as viable options to reduce costs. However, Kumar warns that the company must "make sure that the whole engagement is set up for success, that there is enough sponsorship at the top level and that the initiative has the backing of the senior management. There should be enough communication around it internally to make sure that people are not hugely concerned about job losses and redundancies, etc. So [there] is a strategy in pace to move key people into other areas as appropriate."

CRM is a hot topic at the current moment. However, looking beyond the horizon into life after CRM, Kumar sees the market moving towards a future where the bank becomes "an integral part of the value chain of the client process." The customer is more involved in the end product than ever before. IKEA is given as a successful example: it released part of its value chain, which has been picked up by the customer. By doing this, IKEA has made it easier for people to transport products back home, reduced the company's own operational costs, and passed on those cost benefits to the customers. He observes that more and more companies in India are letting go of part of their value chain through Internet banking and microfinance. Using various technology-enabled techniques, which allow mobile banking and more services to be accessible through multiple channels, there is greater innovation that, in turn, drives customer intimacy.

# *"Don't outsource problems: solve the problems, then outsource your service."*

p75 Kumar expects the CRM drive to eventually move towards a customer-based solution.° This will be more about solving customers' problems than about providing a set of products.

The Internet has made the world a level playing field. Many banks have benefited by "information asymmetry, which creates a situation whereby a higher price premium exists for information that is not easily accessible. Internet technology has given every bank almost the same information. Kumar sees this as a call for innovation and shortening the innovation cycle.

Outsourcing is a topic that no company can afford to ignore. To Kumar, there is a clear-cut answer to the question of whether a company should outsource its strategy or execution excellence: "The standards of services are more about efficiency than scale, and that is [what can be] outsourced to a large extent." Strategic thinking, on the other hand, would not be outsourced because that is part of the bank's core operation and should be retained internally. The bank simply needs to determine what those strategic priorities are before it can search for a a partner "who will ensure that from an execution excellence perspective, it is delivered at the best cost and in the most predictable way." When considering outsourcing, wage inflation is a concern as it has the potential to cancel out the cost benefits of outsourcing in the first place. Kumar does not see wage inflation occurring at all levels. However, he agrees that alternative labour pools need to be recognised. China has rapidly risen to compete with India in the outsourcing race. Both countries have strengths and weaknesses, but Kumar believes that India has an edge over China in terms of language and its young population. Ultimately, the choice is about partners and the successful alignment of the bank's goals with what it is trying to get done. Sharing his insights, Kumar suggests that companies should not look at outsourcing as the answer to their problems. Problems cannot be outsourced; the company itself must first solve them, and then outsource its service.

Kumar talks about the banking legacy environment, which is becoming so complex that the cost of change is quickly becoming prohibitive. "If [the bank] wants to make a small change, the level of regression testing that the bank has to do in order to ensure that that change does not break down something else is more than the cost of development itself." He sees the market moving towards "Core Banking Transformational Projects" as a response to this problem. It entails replacing the core banking platform with a product or products that can help the bank realign its processes to enable greater agility in bringing about change. In coming to terms with these legacy systems, financial services institutions are gradually moving towards becoming more modular. Whatever the technology, the role of the ICT department is to assess these technologies and to offer key inputs into strategic decisions about how the business will continue forward.

JARON LANIER
RABOBANK
FINANCE AS A GAME
I'd play for even NO REWARD!
Most successful WHIZ-KIDS treat finance & investment as a game
WHAT CAN RABOBANK DO TO KEEP THEM GAMING ON?
CREATIVITY & INNOVATION REQUIREMENT
CURRENT LEVEL OF CREATIVITY IS A FUTURE COMMODITY
OUTSOURCING
IS A TOOL for LIMITING LIABILITY & MANAGING COST
a BALANCER of GLOBAL DIFFERENTIALS
COST OF REAL ESTATE X
COST OF REAL ESTATE X-Y
I'll go where it's CHEAP to LIVE!
STRONG
DIVISIO
BETWE
ON THE
FREE LABOUR is cheaper than CHEAP LABOUR
BILL G.
Ooh, I know I know...
HIDING THE TRUE COST OF IT IN "VOLUNTEER DEVELOPE LABOUR
That would be YOU & ME!
Living & learning from SECOND LIFE
It's MY WORLD and it obeys me.
CHARACTERS are
• MULTI-CREATIVE
• EROTIC (HYPER-
• HIGHLY INTERACTIVE
• VIBRANT
The next phase of USER INTERFACE?
Why does money seem MORE REAL in SECOND LIFE than in the REAL LIFE?
CONSUMER
In the WEST, CONSUMERS are STAGE-DIVING off THE TOP OF MASLOW'S HIERARCHY
ACTING on BELIEFS, EXPECTATION of BEING ENTERTAINED
DECELERATING TRENDS affect the FUTURE just as MUCH as accelerating trends
POPULATION GROWS OLDER
→ conservatism
There's not been a NEW STYLE of music for 2 GENERATIONS!
We've GLOBALLY ARRIVED where we're SUPPOSED TO BE
STUCK in and with the TECHNOLOGY
Pattern exhaustion ALL the IDEAS have been USED UP.
We've been ENSLAVED by our TOOLS of IT in music-making!
1. PLATEAU SCENARIO
RECHARGE!
by APP SYSTEM
IT innovation BARELY HAS A PULSE LEFT!

TURBULENCE AHEAD!
THE NEGATIVE SCENARIO 3.
IT DOESN'T DEVELOP
we fall PREY to GLOBAL LOSS of TRUST in the safety & security of IT
IMPROVED COMMUNICATION THRU
RICHER EXPRESSION
EXPLODES the UNDER-STANDING!
FOR CONSUMERS!
VISUALISATION of INFORMATION
EASY-TO-USE-INTERFACES
ANOTHER challenge for BANKERS!
EVERYONE KNOWS & LOVES ME!
VS.
VANITY
ENTERTAINMENT
BANKING look like?
We've got a MUSIC DIRECTOR, EXPERIENCE DIRECTOR & A STUNT-MAN ON THE PAYROLL!
It may be MANDATORY, but why could it not be fun, too?
CREATING a NEW LEVEL of communi-cation!
BREAKTHROUGH SCENARIO
eg SECOND LIFE
much smarter software than most can even imagine
SOFTWARE with instant FEEDBACK & error recognition
LEAP INTO THE NEXT LEVEL
LEARNING
Annika

# Jaron Lanier

## Computer scientist and virtual reality (VR) pioneer

A leading pioneer of virtual reality and a computer scientist, Jaron Lanier shares his concerns about the difficulties of managing ICT systems that have reached increasing levels of complexity. He finds that ICT management is not confronting this complexity, suggesting that "the ICT management task is a little bit beyond the capacity of humans and human groups as we have been able to construe them." Assembling different ICT parts does not simply increase the complexity in direct proportion, but increases it exponentially, leaving ICT professionals ill-prepared to resolve issues. Although Lanier recognises that many interesting and ambitious ideas have resulted in incremental improvements, "the rate of improvement in the quality of the underlying ideas and tools does not match this sort of exponential level of difficulty in managing complexity increases." •

p66
p76

At some time in the future, Lanier predicts, this complexity will reach a point where it will no longer be financially feasible to patch solutions, and fundamental change will be required. He proposes a normative scenario in which human expectations of continuous expansion—in terms of "globalisation, the integration of ICT into the personal lives of people, the further integration of government and industry into a greater levels of complexity and efficiency with giant ICT systems"—will come to a halt.

As a computer scientist, Lanier predicts that there is much room for scientific and mathematical innovation that could lead to much better systems. This entails fundamental reconsiderations of how computers and communication networks are put together. One promising approach is to shift from "the idea of programming a system towards the idea of specifying a system." Lanier describes this approach as one having "a very high-level description of what the system should achieve instead of actually controlling what the logic gates and the chips do with programming languages." The system would then subsequently synthesize its own code.

As a pioneer in the field of virtual reality, Lanier is particularly interested in the implications of massive virtual worlds, such as Second Life, an online virtual world in which people use avatars to interact with one another in a virtual space. "Because of the creative activity that happens within it, [Second Life] has changed the dynamics between people." An interesting idea for Lanier is whether a banking customer will, in 10 years time, be interacting with a bank in a world like this. Since Lanier's interview in 2006, this vision has been realised: financial services providers, such as ABN Amro, BNP Paribas, ING Bank and Wells Fargo have set up shop within Second Life.

# *"We're starting to see a new phenomenon: entertainment banking."*

Lanier suggests a scenario of an ICT catastrophe. It is a scenario in which ICT management does not improve, but demands for more skilled, more complex and more quickly modified ICT systems continue to grow. Because the system cannot be managed, there are some security breaches or other hazards that shake the confidence of consumers. In this unstable world, the role of the bank goes back to its origins. "It becomes almost an institution that is an alternative source of managing life and the future, and an alternative to the state and religion. It p67 becomes almost a source of stability of last resort."•

An opposite scenario to this vision of catastrophe is a world in which medicine can cure all diseases, and human needs are met at every basic level: medicine, nutrition, shelter, etc. In this world of well-being, banking has the potential to become entertainment itself. According to Lanier, an entertainment bank will have some resemblance to Washington Mutual's latest transformation—a bank that has tried to cater to young families in upscale neighborhoods. He finds that the branches reflect "a combination of both the upscale and comfortable and also the desire to be cultural." As the financial sector becomes increasingly associated with entertainment, it is not unlikely for online banking to move completely into virtual spaces, such as Second Life.

Lanier talks about disappearing knowledge margins, a trend that is reinforcing creativity within companies, such as financial services providers. In a capitalistic system, "the way somebody makes money is by having a situational advantage, where they have access to information or intelligence or something else that other people do not have." As the level of communication becomes richer and better, more people understand more things. This leveling of the playing field eats away at traditional sources of margins. The banking system runs the risk of becoming so commoditised that there is no longer any profit, and the sector will find itself in "a kind of arms race of creativity, [where] the old level of creativity becomes commoditised and the customers have access to it, and the seller is forced by the market to become more creative; to offer something more beautiful [and profound] that the customer cannot really put together."

ICT complexity | virtual worlds | entertainment banking | creativity arms race | Lanier

By shaping our own future in the different scenarios in clay, we really became part of the scenario. What had been an interesting story up until that moment became reality while working it out in clay.

Wil Leeuwis

# Peter Leyden

Strategic Network Director & Fellow, New Politics Institute

In 1997, Peter Leyden, a former journalist for *Wired Magazine*, co-authored an article called "The Long Boom" with Peter Schwartz, co-founder and CEO of the Global Business Network, which explored the technology trends of the day, and the spread of digitisation and the Internet. Even after the dot.com boom and bust, Leyden has observed that every single element discussed in that article has remained, and none of those trends has disappeared.

In this era of extended economic expansion, Leyden sees a second wave of broadband Internet, the first wave being the low-bandwidth Internet boom. He describes it as witnessing "an almost inevitable and inextricable adoption of putting this entire [broadband] media onto the Internet." Business models are changing. Television networks that were once staunchly against sharing any shows on the Internet are now making deals with vendors, such as Apple, or streaming their material via the company website.

Equally as influential as the Internet, the digitisation phenomenon has been gradually and quietly providing people with extremely cheap and powerful tools. Leyden believes this phenomenon is extremely important. It puts an unprecedented amount of control in the hands p76 of the consumer.* On the producer side, the cost of production has been reduced dramatically, leading to substantially more professional content, and thus, many more professional players in the market. "Because of the global nature of the Internet and the globalisation of the economy, the bottom-up phenomena actually goes global, so [there is] a whole level of software, which is a little more tailored to outsourcing and to global work-teams." In the bigger picture, everyone's cheap tools are connected via the Internet, and collaboration occurs across the entire infrastructure. This phenomenon starts at the bottom with interconnected users, and trends begin to rise upwards. Leyden does not see bottom-up open source completely replacing top-down processes. Like a pendulum swing, he believes that these two forces will be fundamentally rebalanced.

Discussing the vast amount of liquidity in the world, Leyden suggests that the problem in productivity today is too much money. With a lot of private equity chasing too few deals, prices are driven upwards. financial services and money management have always been about scarce capital, and the sudden oversupply of capital is shifting the capital management paradigm. Leyden proposes that the global challenge of the 21st Century is to find a way to harness that capital. He believes that human capital and financial capital are the two critical assets that must be harnessed to solve this century's problems. Successfully deploying these

# *"The Millennial generation is coming—they'll be the economy in the next 20 years."*

assets would help any company or organisation weather serious disruptions to the global economy, be it a terrorist attack or a global pandemic. Should this occur, financial services institutions would revert to their traditional focus on trust and people.° p67

Leyden observes that there is an ongoing "rebalancing between the developed and developing world in financial capital." He believes that there will be numerous ways to apply capital very productively in emerging markets because of their potential for high growth.

The crux of Leyden's remarks focus on two demographic groups: the Baby Boomers and the Millennials. The Millennials are generally defined as people born roughly between 1980 and 2000, and are the children of the Baby Boomers. Within the United States, a significant portion of the Millennial generation are immigrants. He predicts that by 2050, the ethnic and racial distribution in the United States will be the reverse of the current situation. Of the total population, the white population will constitute less than 50%, the Hispanics, over 35%, and Asians, 8%-10%. The Baby Boomers transformed the United States into a youth culture, and redefined consumption at every level as the Boomers progressed through different stages in life. Similarly, the Millennials are also transforming the world. Their impact is no less than the impact of the Baby Boomers. Their generational characteristics set them apart from older generations. In general, the Millennials are close to their parents, very civic minded, concerned with team building, concerned with the environment, and are ICT proficient. The Millennials are also dealing with issues that are completely different from those of the Baby Boomers. The latter had to fight for gender equality, whereas the Millennials take this issue for granted.

Leyden strongly believes that a bank or business that does not give due consideration to the Millennials is unwise. Within the next 20 years, this generation will essentially be the economy.° p48 In much the same way Baby Boomers have influenced certain markets with their lifestyles, so will the Millennials.

According to Leyden, "Globalisation has created a set of incredibly complex problems, which will either bring the whole thing down or will essentially be solved by innovation and tools of globalisation itself." He believes that everyone is waiting for someone else to figure out the problems. People seek to answer the complexity problem in the form of one person, which, in Leyden's opinion, is "a retro, backward-looking, traditional way of understanding and solving problems." He believes that it is impossible for a single person to provide the solution.

The only way to deal with the current level of complexity is to "distribute systems of nodes among autonomous, intelligent actors who can solve a piece of it." From that point forward, these pieces are aggregated, and collaborative interactions help to build solutions. There is still a real need for leadership, but the key is still with the wisdom of the masses.

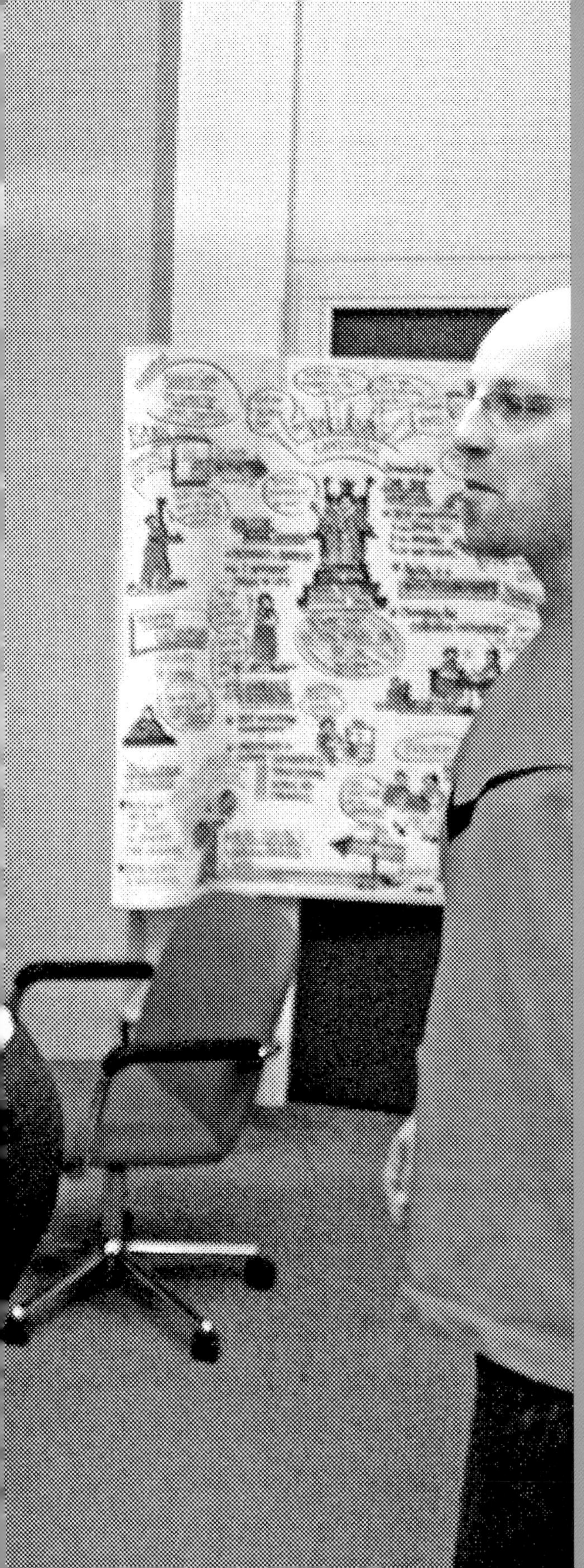

Apart from new insights, the process generated a lot of energy and enthusiasm. Every part of the process was playful and creative. We could never see what would be the result at the end of a session, but at some point the pieces of the puzzle would always come together.

Jeanne Driessen

# Krish Murali Eswar

Founder, MARGAbandhu Consultants; Board member, Trestle Group Foundation

Krish Murali Eswar believes strongly that the future prosperity of a country, its ability to innovate and grow, lies with its people. For Eswar, India has few well-known leading global products, except for its people. He believes that there is a real need for innovation and a support system for that innovation within India to enable the country to better compete in a one-world community. Indians are good in structured thinking. Despite India's assets, Eswar worries that the country does not have a systemic way of combating or understanding the mounting competitive forces in a one-world community. Therefore, he proposes that if India decides to make innovation the key for leading India's economy into the future, innovation itself must be brought to bear in the form of a structured methodology. To realise a vision, Eswar proposes that strategists should look to the strategies for winning wars throughout history because "these are time-tested principles." He does not see India competing on resources, not because the country is resource-poor, but because prosperity is unevenly distributed. "The wisdom of using our resources is just now coming into India." He believes that it will take another few years for this change to come about.

Eswar outlines the key attributes of a successful ICT department for a typical bank. ICT departments should be able to offer banking products quickly to the marketplace. This means that the ICT department services the business needs of the bank. This involves a significant amount of strategic alignment for the ICT department and the business side of the bank. ICT departments need to provide the technological support for the bank to offer better products and services to their customers even as they stay within the allotted budget. ICT departments have not invested in any major technologies for many years. Most of the banking systems that are running today are actually home-grown systems, which have been stabilised over a period of time, and have thus gained confidence. It is easy for ICT departments to continue to rely on these systems because the stability offers a great level of comfort. However, technology has improved much faster than the systems that ICT department budgets can afford. These maturing systems have been retained and sustained for such a long period of time, that the mere sustenance of the system has become a challenge. These so-called legacy systems have now become a white elephant. Because of the expense, Eswar thinks that it will be difficult to make the switch to comply with many of the "emerging standards in the Internet space, in the e-commerce space, p57 and in various spheres of government and other regulations in the global market."*

Another role of the ICT department is to find cheaper and better ways for technology to continue delivering banking products and services. ATMs made it much more convenient for

## *"40% of Oracle is made up of Indians and close to 50% of Microsoft are Indians."*

the customer to handle simple cash transactions, while also reducing the costs of maintaining branches. The next step will be for banks to find some other technology to make it even cheaper to provide such service.

At the root of the matter, financial services institutions have a system that works extremely well in some areas, but in others, it is prone to stagnation, finding it difficult to change, to adapt and to move forward. Hence, according to Eswar, "Banks with large significant current investments and large significant long-running systems with people who have built them and have stood by them for a period of time will look to their own core competency and strength as an advantage over their competitor. Eventually, [however], this will become a kind of barrier."

In order to prepare for potentially harmful forces in the future, the ICT department will try to put processes in place that can help to surmount some of those barriers. "The process is not about building a product; it is about evolving a product over a period of time." Therefore, the ICT department needs to work closely with the business area. This makes this co-creation process heavily people-dependent. At some point, when ICT processes appear to be standardised and stabilised, they can be outsourced. However, in outsourcing, there is the challenge of an "out of sight, out of mind" mentality: since the company cannot see what the worker is doing on a day-to-day basis, the company begins to worry a lot. It takes time for ICT departments to gain trust in offshore centres. One of the largest barriers in a successful outsourcing relationship is the perception of the parent organisation that it will lose control of the service or product being outsourced. This insecurity can be addressed, in most cases, by maintaining a certain level of transparency to enable the parent organisation to continue to feel in control.

Eswar believes that culture will always play a large role in outsourcing relationships. Language, while being a relatively straightforward barrier to overcome, can still be the source of a great many misunderstandings. Cultural attitudes complicate this process of mutual understanding even further. For example, in India and China, there is not a great track record for intellectual property. Although culture is a significant barrier, as long as there is a certain level of adaptability inherent within the culture, it can be part of the solution for resolving cross-cultural communication issues.

Eswar believes that India will go far in the global economy. For instance, Indians are good systematic thinkers with a high degree of adaptability inherent in the culture. Particularly in the

ICT sector, Indians have generally adopted English as the primary language of business, making it easier for Western companies to do business with Indian companies. India is currently a very youthful society. A youthful culture is an important ingredient for innovation and growth because youth possess self-esteem, knowledge, curiosity and an exploratory spirit, leaving them open to taking risks and experimentation. India also has a unique cultural characteristic of very strong cultural bonding, in which "everyone is treated like family." Eswar admits that many Western companies may find it difficult to work successfully with Indians because India is not culturally ready, having been in a global space from a contextual perspective of only 15 years or so. It will take time and adjustment for cross-cultural project processes to smooth out.

Eswar categorizes his ideas into short term, medium term and long term. In the short term, he sees staff augmentation projects gaining momentum. This means that despite rising wages in India, companies will be looking at the talent pool, specific abilities and project size, and control because of a desire for accountability. Solutions-based consulting will emerge from this as more and more players realise that costs are increasing. Business-critical work will remain in-house, but outsourcing companies will increasingly offer a product-based solution or a framework-based solution to help get rid of problems.

p59 In the medium term, Eswar sees the emergence of a tool-based approach. A basic framework addresses 70% of the processes, but it can be adapted to suit the needs. He believes that noncore areas will emerge and continue to be a driver for outsourcing. In the long term, Eswar predicts that "as Indian companies begin to invest in acquiring solution-based, product-based services, India will emerge as global consulting hub." India isn't culturally ready yet, but it will not be long before the country is ready. He also expects the emergence of a new reward model for consulting, describing it as "no cure, no pay services." In this model, a customer presents the bank with a problem. The customer only pays the bank after it has solved it. The payment reflects what the bank seems to deserve and not what the bank desires. Eswar suggests that ICT departments should prepare for the emergence of new delivery channels because customers cannot be expected to continue to come through the Internet, a teleservice of SMS. "New delivery channels through mobile technology will emerge, as well as interactive entertainment channels because there is so much investment going into electronics today." It is obvious to Eswar that the future belongs to anyone who can demonstrate value. How ICT departments in banks will do this is a discussion that will require much thought, planning and preparation.

RABOBANK
ERIC RODENBECK
Founder / Stamen Design
We focus on visualisation of information
MAKING
DATA visible and information self-explanatory
We like to MESS with DATA!
MIX UP the DATA and see WHAT HAPPENS!
LEARNING to "READ" visual information takes some time
Right, like ANY NEW LANGUAGE
Help your customer SEE the
The information needed in RUNNING A SMALL business finances
Your balance sheet shows your books tell
And could I then COMPARE it with SOME-ONE else's DATA?
INSIGHT!
I HAVE seen the LIGHT!
ORACLE QUESTION
What is the NEW E-MAIL for banking?
What BEHAVIOUR is allowed that's not allowed NOW?
What NEW INDUSTRY will banking enable?
How would a CONSUMER DRIVEN bank look?
When's the tipping point for BANKS to dump IE
OPEN SOURCING
Vaccine development in the open source sphere
Open source BANKING doesn't sound very SOLID... maybe SMALL LABS for INNOVATION
DO YOU DARE

"VISUALISATION"
GOOGLE Mapping
should work interactively
ASK questions
ABLE to impact it
LIVE information
information should be FREELY ACCESSIBLE & TRANSFORMABLE by the RECIPIENT
Like PLAY-DOH!
OPENING UP INFORMATION will produce NEW INNOVATIONS
Can you show me my MORTGAGE options
Not MY BANKING DATA, please!
VISUALLY?
Example of FLICKR combining MAPPING TAXOLOGY with LOOSE TAGGING system
Eg MOVE ON
This looks interesting
AND LOOK at this!
RABOBANK data
VISUAL maps built of ORIGINALLY DISCONNECTED PHOTOS by INDIVIDUALS
DEVELOP DEVELOP
TEST TEST
FLUID, DON'T FREEZE IT
CHANGE AND CHANGE

# Eric Rodenbeck

## Founder & Creative Director, Stamen Design

Eric Rodenbeck's business is all about visualisation—the representation of information and data in a visual context that is not static but can be modified. He illustrates the difficulty most people have with interpreting financial data. For example, when initiating a mortgage process, a customer is often presented with a list of numbers that to the untrained eye is essentially meaningless. This sort of data can be presented in a way that is understandable for anyone. It should answer two basic questions, in the context of a mortgage: whether the customer can afford it, and how much the customer will receive.

Rodenbeck states that he has yet to see "the use of data visualisation to impact the data." Currently, he really only sees a data set and then the visualisation of that data set, such as in pie charts or bar graphs. He does not see a way for data visualisation to feed back into the data. He sees may possibilities for data visualisation. He finds open APIs and what people p74 have created from open APIs particularly fascinating, such as Flickr and HousingMaps.com. He believes that one of the ways to foster innovation is to bring hackers into the mix. He feels that banks can leverage this by letting them ask questions about the bank's data that it doesn't think to necessarily provide.

Rodenbeck talks about heat mapping, which is a visualisation tool for large amounts of data. A heat map is composed of different boxes. The size of each box represents the magnitude of the subject. For example, if the heat map is about market capitalisation, then the size of the box will represent the market share of a particular stock. The colours of the boxes represent how well something is doing, or whatever the parameters are.

Despite his support for better data visualisation, Rodenbeck stresses the importance of explanation and understanding. "Just because somebody has better access to their data, [it does not mean] that they are going to start making wiser financial decisions". It will take some time for people to adopt these innovations because people may not begin investigating right away, even with the right tools. Specifically regarding visualisation for banks, Rodenbeck p59 cautions that banks should stay flexible. While banks should definitely look into ways to better visualise data, he does not believe that banks should come up with a big long-term strategy for dealing with the topic because these trends change quickly. He calls it a "release early, release often" strategy whereby the whole process may not be planned all the way through. There is a lot of openness, transparency and experimentation.

## *"How can we manage innovation from small teams of people operating outside the structures they used to need?"*

A supporter of open source systems, Rodenbeck is concerned by proprietary systems, such as Oracle and Microsoft, because of the resistance to innovation and maintenance costs. While some people may dismiss open source as a kind of second dot.com boom, Rodenbeck warns that it should not be dismissed out of hand. In fact, the people who are in this current boom also figured in the last one. Because of their experience with the previous boom-bust cycle, they are much more experienced and realistic. Similar trends are taking place again, and these individuals know where the pitfalls are and how to avoid them. While he finds that banking is a fairly static industry, Rodenbeck also hopes to see Google-like innovation in the industry, with very small teams of people operating outside the banking infrastructure. He feels that that kind of flexibility and openness is where innovation happens.

In his argument for open source, Rodenbeck explains that it is much cheaper because there is no need for such training as Oracle training, and there is no need to buy any software or updates. People can spend more time working and less time getting board certified, which logically, should increase productivity. His vision of open source banking is one that "allows p47 the fostering of dissemination of information."• Whether or not that vision will reach fruition, he believes that, ultimately, flexibility and a willingness to experiment with results-driven people are the key driving forces for innovation.

Learning to think in scenarios makes life easier. That is true for working life as well as for private life. I find that scenario thinking suits me. Who in the end knows the future, and isn't it terribly narrow and scary to pinpoint yourself to one scenario?

Margreet Oostenbrink

Ralph Schonenbach

# Ralph Schonenbach & Severin Weiss

CEO, Trestle Group; Director Switzerland and India, Trestle Group

The Trestle Group is focused on sourcing, covering five different areas: consulting, research, human capital, venture and nonprofit. The consulting practice is by far the largest group. Because of the global spread of the Trestle Group and its business model, the company has a deep understanding of the outsouring model and where it is headed.

Severin Weiss talks about captive centres in India, which are outsourcing companies, owned like subsidiaries. They may be run by local management, but are fully owned by the parent company wherever the parent company is headquartered. He describes captive centres as a "back-office kind of 'body shop' and not really a project-based setup." This means that the turnover for ICT professionals in captive centres is quite high because they may not grow rapidly enough. There are not really challenging projects; in fact, most projects in the Indian ICT industry are application management and maintenance projects. Weiss explains that if a company comes in and decides to focus on the development process, that company can attract talented engineers quite easily. The question that remains is whether or not the company can retain the talent. Captive centres are also threatened by wage increases in India. This is a serious problem within smaller organisations. While they are compelled to increase salaries, they are still unable to attract enough young talent.

When it comes to outsourcing, Weiss relates that he has seen many projects fail in the last few years, but none because of technical reasons. The main reason for their failure was lack of communication. Parent companies need to view their outsourcing partners as "an integrated part of the organisation and more than willing to add value, not just manpower." This can be resolved by establishing a bridge between the parent company and the outsourcing partner. Communication starts with a definition of the project scope. This definition should be flexible enough to allow for adjustments in expectations from both parties. Schonenbach believes that a lot of sourcing or outsourcing relationships break down when neither side sees the relationship as a partnership. Without a two-way channel of communication and understanding, there will be a lot of complications.

Weiss suggests some models of cooperation with outsourcing companies. One of the models is called the "build-operate-transfer" or BOT model, in which the parent company joins or works with a local partner in India. The local partner is responsible for setting up an organisation and recruiting people on behalf of the parent company. The parent company remains in control, having the last word on almost all decisions.

# *"Every system is a legacy system."*

When it comes to software packages, Schonenbach thinks that it is a dream scenario for any large organisation to be able to buy packaged software, plug it in and have everything work without a hitch.• p57 However, because large organisations have many different legacy systems with many different interfaces, this scenario is unlikely to happen without some difficulties. In reality, large organisations, particularly in the banking and insurance industries, have built their own legacy applications over time. Because there are too many applications interfaced to the legacy system, it is too difficult to migrate the entire system to a different platform. However, more and more functionality, brought in as part of software packages, is built in from third-party members. The parent company still needs resources to maintain it. In the end, software packages for large organisations only really means that the company has bought a framework, not a finished package out of a box.

Weiss and Schonenbach propose a scenario whereby Indian banks may begin to buy European banks.• p76 Although this idea may seem strange initially, Schonenbach believes that it is quite possible because there is tremendous growth in India and a lot of accumulated wealth. There is also a lot of cash, which many European banks do not have. The local market in India will see continued growth in the ICT sector. Furthermore, there is a growing entrepreneurial spirit in India. Weiss believes that in the near future, "there will be more 'Bill Gates' in India." Both Schonenbach and Weiss see much potential in India. In Europe, there is a general attitude of risk-aversion. In direct contrast, people in India are unafraid to take risks in pursuit of growth and expansion.

Weiss advises that the parent company needs to be very specific in conveying its needs and requirements when conducting business in India. Usually it is important for local partners to feel committed to a project in order to deliver. He also emphasises that it is important to build up trust, as it establishes a better foundation for cooperative partnerships. Weiss is uncertain about whether it is a wise option for a European bank to participate directly in India. He believes that the cultural differences are too great in every industry, and that it would be a major challenge for any European bank. However, it is feasible for a European bank to enter the Indian market through joint ventures or some other partnership model.

Schonenbach and Weiss express concern about where new customers for the financial services industry will come from. They are less concerned about the relevance of ICT in the future. ICT will evolve with the business; identifying the source of future business growth is seen to be of greater importance. Schonenbach predicts that information will become a new product in banks. This means that people will have "an information account in their private bank, and it will be the bank's responsibility to keep this secure, to provide access, and to allow people to use this information in a productive way. [The person] who owns information controls the world." Being able to manage that information will be the next great challenge.

For now, India is primarily delivering ICT products and services. However, Weiss predicts that this will soon change, as indicated by requests for better jobs and more challenging work. Eventually, there may be a shift in the centre for ICT innovation, moving away from India to another country.

Weiss predicts that in 10 years' time, there will not be enough young people in Europe and there will be a shortage of highly skilled people. The next step will be to outsource, but at some point, that will also change. The more sustainable option would be to attract talent, wherever this talent may be found, whether within Europe or outside of it.

Schonenbach notes that there is often a focus on cost for the CEO of a company. Personally, he feels that the more important and relevant question is how to increase revenue. His belief is that when the discussion moves from finding ways to reduce costs to looking for ways to increase revenue, the company starts seeking opportunities for growth. In other words, the company looks outward rather than inward. Inward focus tends to narrow a company's vision, whereas expanding that focus enables a company to spot both opportunities and threats.

# RAJEEV SRIVASTAVA
## APAR / CEO & Co-founder

RABOBANK

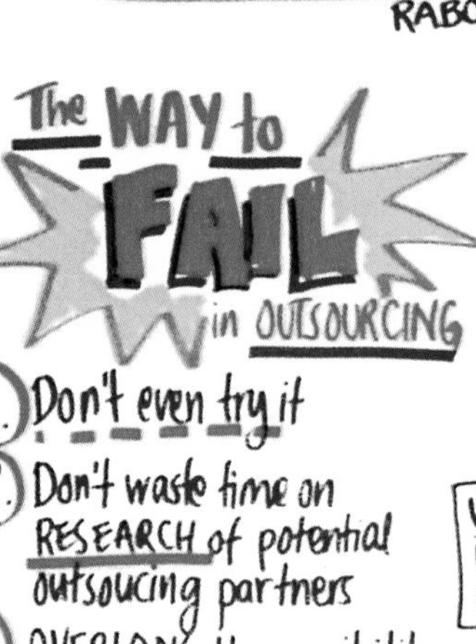

1. Don't even try it
2. Don't waste time on RESEARCH of potential outsoucing partners
3. OVERLOOK the possibility of EQUITY EXCHANGE

We're not interested in CAPITAL GAINS. So.

4. Only examine BIG PLAYERS, as the smaller, new companies might offer too brilliant opportunities for investment
5. Avoid EQUITY STAKES as that would INCREASE your CONTROL, too.

We don't NEED to worry about KEEPING OUR CORE CAPABILITIES SECRET because WE'RE SO GOOD!

6. Go for a controlling interest and START a SUBSIDIARY

Because we have the MONEY to PAY MORE for it!

7. Only ever look for ways to SAVE MONEY, NOT to MAKE money

Yes, that would be IMMORAL & GREEDY.

## RISING COSTS of skilled LABOR

OUTSOURCING is a tempting FIELD. China & Middle-East are RISING,

Philippines is entering the market...

- the higher the skill level, the HIGHER the COST

...but there's still a BIG GAP

Yes, it's SLAVE LABOR!

- ADAPTING to Competition

In-depth und[erstanding] of [the] PARTNER'S CU[...] is neces[sary]

INCREASE LEVEL of SERVICE

TAKE full advantage of ENGLISH Skills

- CONSOLIDATION AHEAD!

Plenty of OPPORTUNITIES!

- Indian companies acquiring also in Europe & USA

GLOBAL PRESENC[E]

Having a TRULY GLOBAL company structure is the ENTRY TICKET for the MAJOR LEAGUE

ORACLE QUESTION
How BIG a ROLE will ICT play in financial industry?
What's the % of EXPENDITURE?
Will PHYSICAL BANKING disappear?
Why SHOULD I use CASH?
How much of TRUST is tied to "PHYSICAL"?
A BIG, SERIOUS BUILDING = TRUST
OR DOES IT?
ON INTERNET, INFORMATION creates SENSE of SECURITY
But surely the LOOK & FEEL & FUNCTIONALITY also affect SENSE of SECURITY
The winner is the one with the most EASILY APPLICABLE information!
How will the NICHE players and BOUTIQUE BANKING play out?

# Rajeev Srivastava

**Co-founder & CEO, Apar Infotech Corp.**

Entrepreneur Rajeev Srivastava has a record of turning small companies into fairly large-sized entities with multimillion dollar businesses. In this interview, he shares his thoughts on outsourcing and the Indian market.

Outsourcing is the standard solution for companies seeking to reduce their ICT costs, particularly if they are doing development work in either the United States or Europe. Srivastava explains that the most simple and standard method of outsourcing is to look for an outsourcing partner. India has emerged as a preeminent destination for offshoring work p76 in the last few years, particularly in the ICT and BPO industries. That model has evolved, and organisations now prefer to take significant equity positions in those companies that they are doing offshore work with. This is not likely with the top firms in India because those companies will not easily part with equity money. Therefore, for this new model to work, parent companies need to identify players that could be the top companies in the future. Once a partnership is formed, the parent company could take a controlling stake, but there would not be much of an equity gain. The company in India would literally become a subsidiary of the parent corporation. "When you operate under a different name and do not have a majority control of the equity, many of the competing companies would give the newly created subsidiary ICT work, which would then bring both companies serious equity gains.

"India faces competition on the ICT front, particularly from China. China is keen on making serious investments in the ICT software industry, and if it continues to make progress on the language barrier, which is where India still holds an edge, then China will prove to be a serious competition for outsourcing contracts. This situation is not improved by the fact that salary costs alone are rising nearly 15% to 20% every year in India. Although the cost of doing work in India is still around $21 to $22 an hour, and thus much lower than in Europe and in the United States, it is still uncertain whether these costs will eventually match American or European cost structures. In any event, it cannot be dismissed that it is still 20% to 30% cheaper to do business in China than in India. For now, however, India still holds the lead. Since India has been in the game for a longer period of time, it has adapted and tried to bridge the cultural divide. Adaptability and staying ahead of the competition is crucial to a business."

Srivastava predicts that larger companies will be able to adapt both to the economies of scale and investments in productivity. Bigger companies are going to make significant investments in technologies, which should enable them to continue to do well. In contrast, smaller companies

*"Outsourcing succeeds if there is significant involvement and travel between partners."*

are going to find it difficult. Although smaller companies can still compete with bigger companies based on price, if they do not have the same technological investments in place, the market will see a consolidation trend emerging. Consolidation will not only occur within a country, but will cross borders. For Srivastava, it is not unlikely for a trend to emerge where Indian companies aggressively acquire European companies, especially if costs in India continue to go up. Indian companies will have no choice but to adapt by hiring local Americans or Europeans.

Srivastava raises several questions: What will the new cutting-edge technology be? What new technologies will change banking? Will banking ever move completely online and disappear in the physical aspect? As faster, cheaper, wireless, videoconferencing facilities continue to
p59 improve, banking should become much less physical than it is today.* Differentiation among banks will drive more from the services that the bank can offer on the web or other wireless technologies. Making the effort to physically visit a branch is time-consuming for most people, and almost everyone is short on time these days. So it is possible for banks to reduce their physical presence, but it is unlikely that bank branches will completely fade away.

The key to successful outsourcing is keen and intimate involvement, particularly on the cultural side. "There needs to be people from both sides—the outsourcing partner who is permanently positioned there to understand the cultural dynamics of the whole software development, and at the same time, people from [the parent company], so that there is complete transparency." Transparency is particularly important because transparency establishes trust, and trust is crucial, especially when working through cross-cultural issues.

ICT companies and ICT departments need to keep several things in mind. Talent is retained within a company by understanding the needs of ICT employees. If the aspirations of ICT employees are not addressed, they will leave. Attrition is becoming a problem, especially in smaller companies, partly because costs in India keep rising. ICT companies need to take their social responsibility seriously. Investing in communities brings returns in the future in the form of better educated citizens with talent and skills.

The scenario process is mainly aimed at developing different futures together. But it is a perfect environment for team building as well. We started as a relatively new team. Through the discussions we learned each other's opinions and way of thinking, thus getting to know each other intensively.

Sjaak Oosterveer

# Fred Studer

Vice President of Industries & Applications Marketing, Oracle Corp.

As Group Vice President of Oracle Corporation, Fred Studer's responsibilities involve "looking at the marketplace and identifying what the biggest areas of opportunities for Oracle are, considering trends in the industry front through many different verticals and subverticals, looking at different horizontal markets such as the CRM or things like incentive compensation, both regionally and globally." As a company, Oracle is trying to shift its vision to look beyond the next six months to what will happen in the next three years. Studer sees cost containment continuing indefinitely, but at the same time, he sees a resurgence of growth. He finds the financial services industry leaning towards automating businesses, which means that banks will need to maintain costs. However, the main driver for the next three to five years, in Studer's opinion, is "going to be absolute growth, either organically through net new sales and innovation in products, or through inorganic growth which would mean acquiring new companies and getting into different product lines." To bring this about, Studer suggests three primary focus areas: consolidation and the implications around consolidation; content p57 management; and knowledge management.

Oracle is convinced about the importance of open source. According to Studer, "Oracle strives not only to innovate and provide customers with a great valuable product, but also tries to do it below its total possible cost". Open source is a way for Oracle to look at "identifying easier and less expensive ways for its customers to access information and to leverage database technology as well as applications". How open source affects Oracle's business model and whether it will change is unclear. For now, however, the main growth driver for companies is innovation. In Studer's opinion, this involves looking at new customer acquisitions and at getting the most out of current customer bases. Depending on the company's core competency and drivers for new growth, companies will go through changes. These changes are happening more and more quickly. Studer is optimistic that if a system is in place that is "flexible enough to incrementally change these different power points, [the company] will be able to adapt much more quickly to maximise investments in very specific focal areas."

# Anthony Townsend

Research Director, Institute for the Future



As Research Director for the Institute for the Future, Anthony Townsend works in the Technology Horizons program, which takes five- to 10-year locator emerging technologies in a variety of different areas. With regards to the financial services sector, he sees a number of forces that are pushing towards larger frameworks for privacy. To a certain degree, Townsend agrees that banks may be considered experts in managing and securing digital identity and digital processing, but he also thinks that it is unwise to do so as there are no threats or challenges. The biggest challenge for Townsend is that "people want to share aspects of that digital identity with trusted parties, but the variety is exploding." Managing that trust is the challenge; and that presents an opportunity for banks to step in and, in a move similar to eBay's, "monetise that role p66 of being a trusted party in that transaction."

Townsend predicts that mobile payment systems will generate a great deal of conflict because "mobile payment systems will not just be capable of tracking what people are buying, but it will be another way of getting at their location." Although these systems are most advanced in Korea and Japan because of government support, there are definite privacy concerns. The only true benefit to customers of mobile payment systems is convenience. Whether that convenience is worth the concerns of privacy is a different issue.

To Townsend, financial management for the next generation is very complex. This generation is burdened with record levels of consumer debt, at least in the United States. Additionally, many things that used to be taken care of by the state, such as retirement, are no longer luxuries that can be expected. The majority of the American workforce is now actively engaged in planning their own retirement. There is, therefore, a real need for financial management counseling. Townsend believes there are few financial solutions available for this generation, and thus, it is really struggling. "The banking industry basically has, for the most part, removed that personal relationship with the everyday consumer," except for the high-net-worth segment. These people are going to need a lot of "very carefully crafted customised solutions."

p59 Townsend sees a definite opportunity for banks to evolve into an effective digital assistant. The digital assistant model refers to a digital financial assistant that will answer specific queries, or in a more proactive model, actually intervene at certain points.

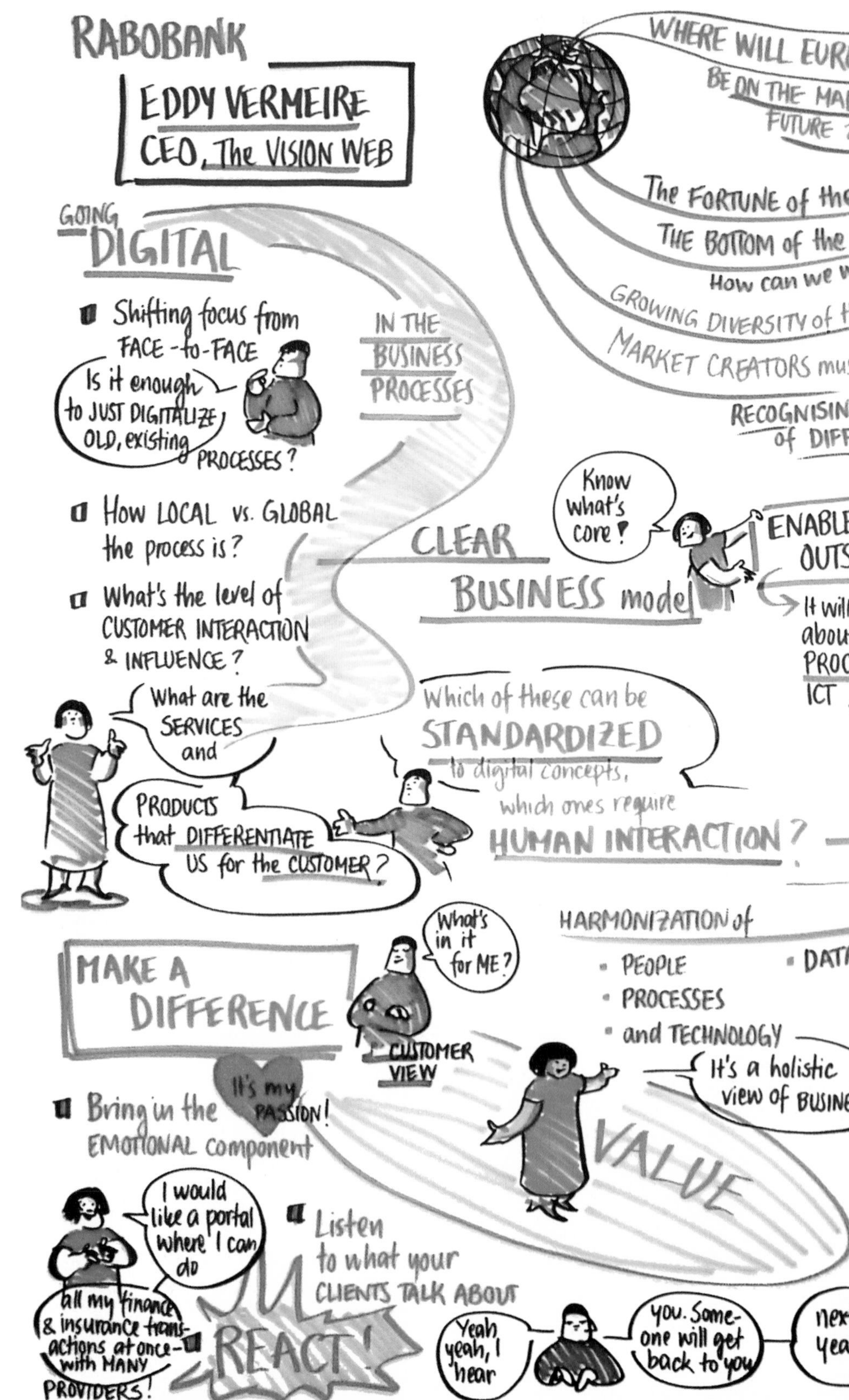
RABOBANK
EDDY VERMEIRE
CEO, The VISION WEB
GOING DIGITAL
Shifting focus from FACE-to-FACE
Is it enough to JUST DIGITALIZE OLD, existing PROCESSES?
IN THE BUSINESS PROCESSES
How LOCAL vs. GLOBAL the process is?
What's the level of CUSTOMER INTERACTION & INFLUENCE?
What are the SERVICES and
PRODUCTS that DIFFERENTIATE US for the CUSTOMER?
Which of these can be STANDARDIZED to digital concepts, which ones require HUMAN INTERACTION?
Know what's core!
CLEAR BUSINESS model
ENABLE OUTSC
It will b about PROCE ICT
WHERE WILL EURO BE ON THE MAP FUTURE?
The FORTUNE of the
THE BOTTOM of the
How can we w
GROWING DIVERSITY of th
MARKET CREATORS must
RECOGNISING of DIFF
HARMONIZATION of
PEOPLE
PROCESSES
and TECHNOLOGY
DATA
It's a holistic view of BUSINES
VALUE
MAKE A DIFFERENCE
What's in it for ME?
CUSTOMER VIEW
Bring in the EMOTIONAL component
It's my PASSION!
I would like a portal where I can do
all my finance & insurance trans-actions at once - with MANY PROVIDERS!
REACT!
Listen to what your CLIENTS TALK ABOUT
Yeah yeah, I hear
you. Some-one will get back to you
next year

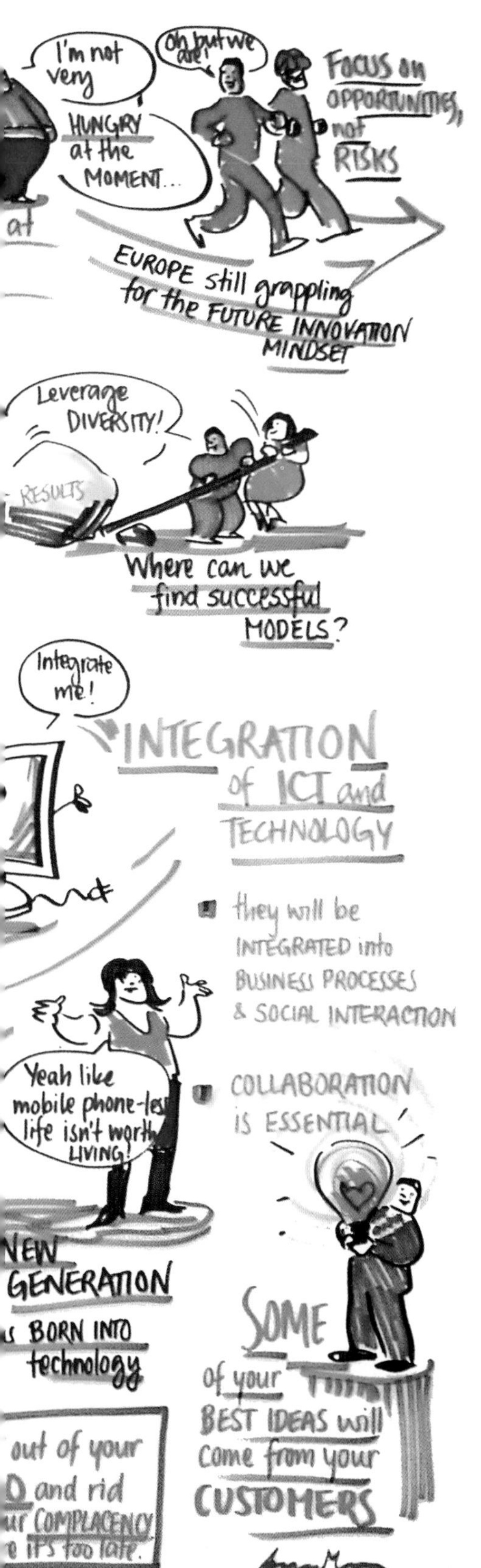

I'm not very
HUNGRY at the MOMENT...
oh but we are!
FOCUS on OPPORTUNITIES, not RISKS
EUROPE still grappling for the FUTURE INNOVATION MINDSET
Leverage DIVERSITY!
RESULTS
Where can we find successful MODELS?
Integrate me!
INTEGRATION of ICT and TECHNOLOGY
they will be INTEGRATED into BUSINESS PROCESSES & SOCIAL INTERACTION
COLLABORATION IS ESSENTIAL
Yeah like mobile phone-less life isn't worth LIVING!
NEW GENERATION
BORN INTO technology
SOME of your BEST IDEAS will come from your CUSTOMERS
out of your
and rid
COMPLACENCY
too late.

# Eddy Vermeire

CEO, The Vision Web

According to Eddy Vermeire, as new digital players enter the market, old structures fade in importance.• p48 p73 If a bank director is asked which is more important, the ATM or the counter where customers are received, the bank director is likely to answer that the importance of the counter is beginning to be questioned. The bank's role in the past was as a repository for money received and taken out. Digitising processes is changing that traditional role. The bank should be fundamentally rethought and redesigned in terms of complexity and in terms of adding new products and services.

Amid the mounting complexity, the bank's service concept is no longer clear. Vermeire believes that if the business service concept is unclear, then so is the role of ICT in banks. Some people feel that ICT is no longer a skill, but something that is standardised. ICT no longer adds to the differentiation of bank services. To Vermeire, when processes are standardised, only two forms of differentiation are left: differentiation in terms of products, and differentiation in terms of services.

In the longer term, if technology is not standardised, then the bank will continue to have a shortage of people with this kind of expertise, fewer suppliers that can deliver these capacities, and increasing complexity. Delivering continuity of service will become an issue eventually, making standardised packages essential to continued service delivery. The back office must also make its business model explicit and well-defined. ICT has a lot of problems because of the lack of definition of the business model. In Vermeire's opinion, ICT must have a role in sourcing and in architecture. People inside ICT departments will need much more business knowledge and an understanding of what truly adds value and what does not in order to weather an increasingly complex future.

Vermeire notes that differentiation in products and services was originally meant for older, high net worth clients. But, as these clients age, there will be fewer growth opportunities from this segment. Vermeire believes that the real growth opportunities are at the bottom of the economic pyramid. People at the bottom of the pyramid do not require complex products. There the banks will also find and retain the youth market. The first phase of personal financial planning starts at youth, and since people really need to organise their own finances, banks play an important role in this development. "It is a whole different approach when you are trying to do things as cheaply as possible. You cannot really base everything on the current system and current processes. You have to think about redefining all of it. If you think

## *"Increasingly, the financial services client will determine his or her own set of priorities."*

about what kind of people you need, what kind of businesses you need to deliver, then that is a fundamentally different approach ... Differentiation is really giving value out of making a difference." In order to deliver on this, all of the bank's services need to work together to deliver value. Therefore, the bank should fundamentally rethink how to deliver, combine and integrate all the various levels of service and cease thinking in terms of silos. The integration of process, data and people, and collaboration among these elements, are essential.

Vermeire agrees that consumer preferences are changing. Consumers need an emotional tie. p73 They want fast responses. Banks are currently not addressing these needs. They are likely to discover that consumers are willing to pay a premium as long as their needs are anticipated and met. Vermeire advises banks to think about what makes sense and respond in terms of service, and to organise an entirely new paradigm from the perspective of the client. Rather than optimising bank processes, Vermeire suggests optimising client services.

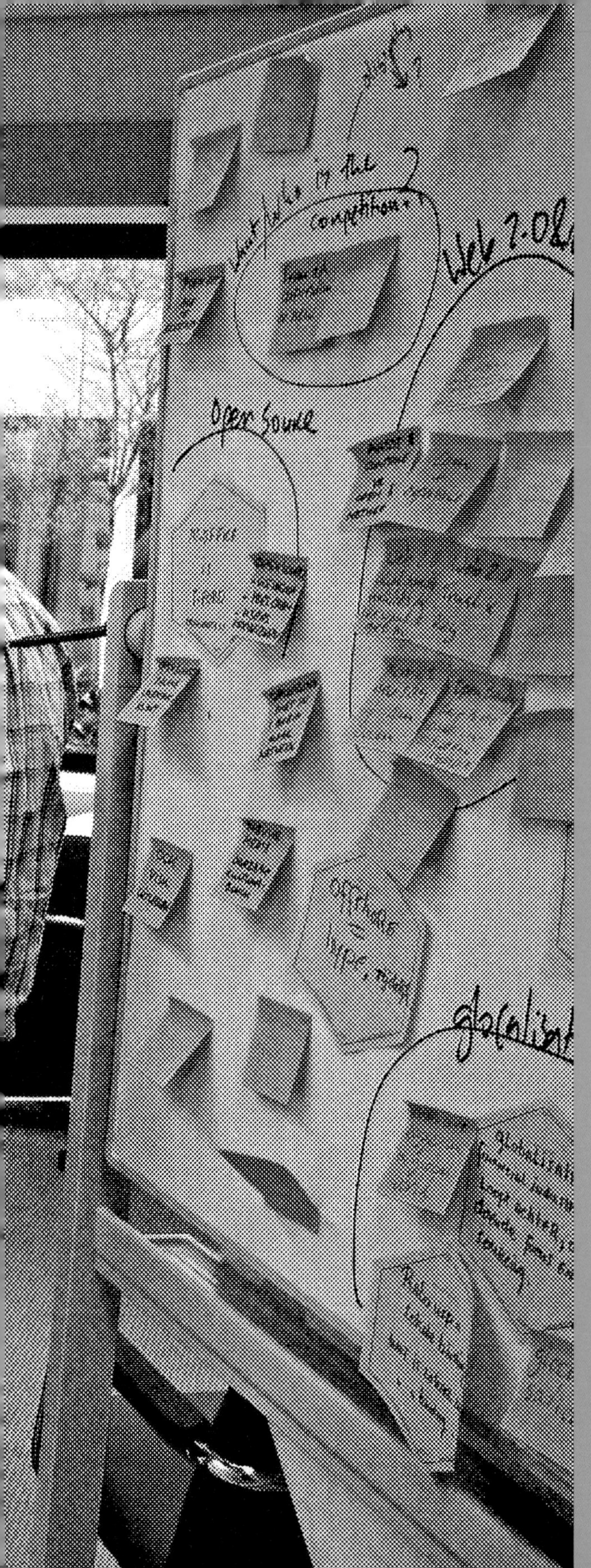


**The scenarios have already proven their worth. Thanks to this process we had already foreseen some recent developments in ICT in financial services.**

Rob Bakker

Chapter 7

# Postscript: From memory of the future to strategic initiatives

**This section focuses on the strategic initiatives that followed the scenario trajectory. Because much of the material is confidential, we cannot give the reader a complete view of the organisation's responses to these possible futures.**

## Hope through hype

Has the role of ICT in enabling financial services in 2017+ been defined? At the outset of the scenario process, the central assumption at Rabobank was that ICT has matured to a point where it can be managed in a traditional bureaucratic way. ICT was therefore almost devoid of innovation. The belief was that software development would be outsourced, and the integrated software providers would finally deliver on the promise of standardised interconnected packages. The future role of an ICT department would be to orchestrate these processes.

The scenario process questioned these assumptions by matching these perceptions with the ICT hype cycle. The IT industry is unique in that it is able to address a new class of problems every decade or so. The key enabler for this has been the doubling of processing power approximately every 18 months. Effectively, we were at the end of ICT hype cycle.

## A crisis of confidence

When we defined the scenarios in 2006, a crisis of globalisation (Geert Mak) seemed very unlikely. Our thinking was much more centred on the possibilities of consolidation (Citi banking scenario) or consumer-focused financial services (Louis Vuitton scenario). We decided to explore the scenario of interconnected risk and the resultant crisis of globalisation (and therefore a financial crisis) from one of the drivers described in the driving forces section—a bird flu pandemic. In June 2006, we discussed the possibility of a financial crisis sparked by a crisis of confidence, based on the securitised assets of subprime mortgages.

What we learned in the June 2006 workshop was: because of the highly leveraged positions in the financial services industry, the high levels of personal debt in the United States, and the interconnected risk in the financial systems, any of a number of events could trigger a global financial crisis. We discussed Rabobank ICT's strategic responses to these scenarios in some depth, both in 2006 and in late 2007, when we felt that our investment options in outsourcing, etc., were not significantly threatened by this potential crisis.

The purpose of the discussion is not to predict an issue, but to see what the implications are of a possible future with respect to our present actions.

## Bedevilled if you do, bedevilled if you don't

In 2006, an important issue for financial services providers in the Netherlands was whether to outsource all of their ICT or part of their ICT, and if they did so, which part?

The scenario interviews in India informed the participants about the outsourcing process. What we realised was that offshoring is not just cutting costs, it is using the huge potential of highly educated and highly skilled IT knowledge workers in India. Rabobank developed a unique outsourcing strategy with the sale of its ICT development division to Ordina. It created a win-win situation between Indian and Dutch ICT professionals and enabled an increase in income as well as a new strategic scope—not just a reduction of costs.

Scenario thinking enables executives to be more reflective in configuring complex decisions because the uncertainties in the external environment are known.

## What stares back?

A good scenario set often questions the foundations of an organisation's business case. In most cases, an organisation avoids thinking through its own death. Basic business models, fundamental to the organisation's survival, remain unquestioned. The scenarios question the foundational role that banks currently play in the flow of capital.

Rabobank is currently exploring peer-to-peer banking through a pilot programme. The question is not whether peer-to-peer banking will replace banks in the future—there are many reasons why it would fail—but that Rabobank is in a position to learn from this new approach to financial services.

## Data on top

ICT systems are getting larger and more complex every year. There is an end to this dynamic, where it will cost so much more to maintain the legacy systems than to develop new functionality. The obvious solution is to address this problem through cheaper development or maintenance. However, this simply delays the inevitable. Another approach stemming from the scenario learning is to fundamentally rethink the development and architecture process.

This is not just a different approach to architecture, but a new way of thinking about data, openness, computing and how to create robust, reliable systems.

## Communication

A key failing of the process was that the scenario thinking exercise did not involve more people. Many of the managers who were central to the process have now moved into new positions. In retrospect, we should have anticipated this and involved a broader group of managers in the thinking process.

I do not believe that the core scenario group should be open, but rather that the borders should be softer. The key critique of the process design presented in this book is that the application of the conclusions are now less likely because it has not become the way of thinking for the larger top-management group. In the future we should design parallel processes to facilitate this process better.

## Conclusion

The above issues are not complete, but they provide some ideas as to how scenarios can challenge an organisation's strategy to innovate more, to cancel projects or to move in a different direction. What is important is not that the scenarios anticipated external events, but that strategic language was developed as the team thought through these issues and tried to understand their implications for the current strategy.

What, then, is the future role of ICT in financial services provision?

Simply put, it is to be a mature discussion partner: a partner that looks beyond the hype with insight into the underlying forces, as well as the opportunities and threats that the external environment will bring. What the answer will be depends largely on influences external to the individual financial services providers. In the financial services industry, Rabobank is unique in raising these questions, even if it doesn't have an answer. The scenarios give us a framework to see in what direction we should look for the answers, and they provide the opportunity to prepare for the different possibilities by planning further ahead than our competitors. But more importantly, the scenarios enable us to look further ahead than our internal and external customers—in order to serve them better.

For the coming five years, the financial services industry will be talking about things that we have raised in these scenarios, leaving us with fewer or no surprises to deal with, and hopefully prepared to anticipate our role better.

Daniel Erasmus
Mumbai 2008

It is great that we are making a book out of this process. This way, we will finally be able to really explain to others what it was we did all this time.

Rob Bakker

Chapter 8

# Sources



## Introduction to scenario thinking


Bell, W. **Foundations of Futures Studies: History, Purposes and Knowledge.** Transaction Publishers: New Brunswick (U.S.A.) and London (U.K), 2007.

Erasmus, D. **"Mastering information management: A common language for Strategy."** *The Financial Times*, 5 April 1997.

de Geus, A. **"Planning as learning."** *Harvard Business Review*, March-April 1998.

van der Heijden, **K. The Sixth Sense.** John Wiley & Sons: Chichester, 2002.

Ingvar, D. **"Memories of the future: an essay on the temporal organisation of conscious awareness."** *Journal of Human Neurobiology* 1985: 4(3).

Wack, P. **"Scenarios: uncharted waters ahead."** *Harvard Business Review*,1985: 63(5).

Wack, P. **"Scenarios: Shooting the rapids."** *Harvard Business Review* 1985, 63(6).


## Key uncertainties of today's global banking environment


**"Banking beyond borders: Will European consumers buy it?"** KPMG, July 2004.

Berger, A. N. **"Global integration in the banking industry."** Federal Reserve Bulletin, November 2003.

Blau, J. "**SaaS still unable to deliver what the enterprise really needs—business processes that are competitive differentiators."** November 2005.
http://weblog.infoworld.com/techwatch/archives/004504.html

Boutitie, E. **"Europe's aging population: the implications for pensions."** *Paribas*, June 1997.

Browning, E.S. "**As boomers retire, a debate: will stock prices get crushed?"** *Wall Street Journal*,May 2005.
http://www.post-gazette.com/pg/05125/499581.stm

Cagni, P. **"Think global, act European."** enews, August 2004.
http://www.strategy-business.com/enewsarticle/enews0830004?pg=all&tid=230

Canfield, B. **"What's next? Top ICTO trends for 2006."** 2005.
http://www.outsourcing-requests.com/center/jsp/requests/print/story.jsp?

Columbus, L. **"Fuel for CRM mergers and acquisitions: maintenance revenues."** May 2005.
http://www.crmbuyer.com/story/43074.html

Dymski, G. **The global bank merger wave: implications for developing countries.** December 2002.

**"Emerging affluent baby boomers, financial services, & the web."** Celent, June 2005.
http://www.celent.com/PressReleases/20050623/BabBoomers.htm

Farrell, D. **"The economic impact of an aging Europe."** McKinsey Quarterly, May 2005.
http://www.mckinseyquarterly.com/article_print.aspx?L2=7&L3=10&ar=1613

Farrell, D. **"Solutions for the demographic deficit."** *Banker*, May 2005.
http://www.thebanker.com/news/printpage.php/aid/2785/Solutions_for_the_demographic_deficit.html

Fisher, L. **"E-commerce and financial services."** January 2001.
http://www.accaglobal.com/publications/fsr/57/1732

**"The future of financial services—changing times."** EMCC, 2003.

**"GLBA and the finance industry."** ArticSoft.
http://www.articsoft.com/gramm_leach_bliley.htm

He, H. **"What is service-oriented architecture?"** O'Reilly, September 2003.
http://webservices.xml.com/pub/a/ws/2003/09/30/soa.html

**"Hong Kong broadband launches 1 Gbps home service for $215/mth."** *Converge*, April 2005.
http://www.convergedigest.com/Bandwidth/newnetworksarticle.asp?ID=14545

Howarth, F. **"Basel II compliance: another burden for European."** CSOs, August 2005.
http://www.it-director.com/article.hp?articleid=12854

Huefner, M. **"Immigration—what Europe can learn from the United States."** *Globalist*, February 2005.
http://www.theglobalist.com/DBWeb/StoryId.aspx?StoryId=4369

van Impe, M. **"Western European mobile banking stalls."** May 2003.
http://www.mobile.commerce.net/print.php?story_id=3143

**"Information visualisation."** Wikipedia.
http://www.ipsos-na.com/news/pressrelease.cfm?id=2583

Kaplan, J. **"Sorting through software as a service."** *Network World*, November 2005.
http://www.networkworld.com/columnists/2005/112105kaplan.html

Lamong, N. **"Remittances are effective weapons against poverty."** Yale Online, November 2005.
http://yaleglobal.yale.edu/display.article?id=6534

Lindquist, C. **"True grid."** *CIO Magazine*, May 2005.
http://www.cio.com/archive/051504/grid.ht ml?printversion=yes

MacEntee, K. & Mackman, B. **"The payments infrastructure must evolve."** November 2005.
http://www.gtnews.com/article/6164.cfm

MacErlean, N. **"Tesco grabs biggest share of new personal finance market."** *Observer*, July 2005.
http://observer.guardian.co.uk/print/0,3858,521782-102271,00.htmlm-banking/e-commerce

Markiewicz, P. **"Who's filling Gen-Y's shoes?"** Brand Channel, May 2003.
http://www.brandchannel.com/print_page.asp?ar_id=156§ion=main

McCue, A. **"Oracle's Siebel buy won't affect us."** *CIOJury*, September 2005.
http://www.silicon.com/ciojury/0,3800003161,39152271,00.htm

McGann, R. **"Broadband: high speed, high spend."** ClickZ Stats January 2005.
http://www.clickz.com/stats/sectors/broadband/article.php/3463191

Mears, J. **"Is security ripe for outsourcing?"** *Network World*, August 2004.
http://www.networkworld.com/news/2004/082304outsecure.html

Modi, N. **"The majority of global internet users using a high-speed connection."** Ipsos News Center, March 2004.
http://www.ipsos-na.com/news/pressrelease.cfm?id=2583

**"On-demand CRM applications market earns leading vendors revenue and commanding market positions."**
IDC, September 2005.
http://www.idc.com/getdoc.jsp?pid=23571113&containerid=prUS00230805

O'Reilly, T. **"What is Web 2.0—design patterns and business models for the next generation of software."**
September 2005.
http://www.oreillynet.com/lpt/a/6228

**"The net impact of thin clients."** 3com, 2000.
http://www.pulsewan.com/data101/thin_client_basics.htm

Rahman, W. & Priya, K. **"European payments—time to step up to the customer challenge."** Infosys August 2005.

**"Service-oriented architecture (SOA)"** definition. Barry & Associates.
http://www.service-architecture.com/webservices/articles

Shuck, J. **"Shifting sources of value in financial services outsourcing."** 2005.
http://www.outsourcing-requests.com/center/jsp/requests/print/story.jsp?id=4810

Sinrod, E.J. **"Let's say 'go phish' to information phishers."** October 2004.
http://www.usatoday.com/tech/columnist/ericjsinrod/2004-10-13-sinrod_x.htm

Stout, K. L. **"Dialing up to do business."** March 2005.
http://www.cnn.com/2005/TECH/03/31/spark.mobile.banking

**"Transforming the financial services industry."** GTNews, November, 2005.
http://www.gtnews.com/article/6168.cfm

Wakeham, J., Hogan, A. & Nelson, H. **"European payment service providers: a race to market."** July 2005.
http://www.gtnews.com/article/ 6031.cfm

## Driving forces: Shaping the future

**"Age: 2000."** U.S. Census Bureau, October 2001.
http://www.census.gov/population/www/index.html

Anderson, M. **"Saving the planet with Plan B."** Wired News, 22 March 2006.
http://www.wired.com/news/politics/lifescience 70455-0.html?tw=rss.politics

**"Asia VOIP market to grow by 1 billion used per year 2005–2009."** AFX News Limited, *Forbes*, 19 February 2006.
http://www.forbes.com/technology/feeds/afx/2006/02/19/afx2538453.html

**"Bankless banking."** *The Economist*, 23 February 2006.

Blomert, L. & de Vries, A. **"Prevalence of Dyslexia in the Netherlands."** 2004.
http://www.bdainternationalconference.org/2004/presentations/mon_s5_c_8.shtml

Boyd, D. **"Why Web 2.0 matters: preparing for glocalisation."** 5 September 2005.
http://www.zephoria.org/thoughts/archives/2005/09/05/why_web20_matte.html

Bremmer, I. **"Taking a brick out of BRIC: Russia doesn't belong in the same league as Brazil, India, and China."** *Fortune*, 7 February 2006.
http://money.cnn.com/magazines/fortune/fortune_archive/2006/02/20/8369169

van Broekhoven, R. **"The day the dollar falls."** VPRO, 20 November 2005.
http://www.vpro.nl/programma/tegenlicht/afleveringen/24877874

Chatterjee, M.B. **"Bangalore to remain top choice for commercial space next year."** The Hindu Business Line, 21 December 2005.
http://www.thehindubusinessline.com/2005/12/22/Stories/2005122202840900.htm

**"China may cut US debt holdings."** BBC News, 4 April 2006.
http://news.bbc.co.uk/1/hi/business/4875606.stm

**"China market, multinationals' paradise?"** *China Business Weekly*, 20 February 2006.
http://www.chinadaily.com/cn/english/dc/2006-02/20/content_521781.htm

**"Compliance: European firms lag on Sarbannes-Oxley."** The Financial Executive, November 2004.
http://www.allbusiness.com/periodicals/article/258337-1.html

Degryse, H., Ongena, S. & Penas, M. F. **"Between Lisbon and London: Financial sector consolidation in the context of the Lisbon Agenda."** December 2005.

**"Discontinuance of M3."** Federal Reserve, 10 November 2005, 9 March 2006.
http://www.federalreserve.gov/releases/h6/discm3.htm

Escobar, P. **"Selling China to the world."** *Asia Times*, 15 January 2005.
http://www.atimes.com/atimes/China/GA15Ad01.html

**"EU mulls budget crisis warning over baby boomers."** EU Business, 13 February 2006.
http://www.eubusiness.com/Finance/060213163534.i41mz8ig

**"EU warning to prepare for retiring boomers."** *International Herald Tribune*, 13 February 2006.
http://www.iht.com/articles/2006/02/13/business/ibrief.php

Euractive. **"What role for financial services in a revamped Lisbon Agenda?"** Euractive, 31 January 2006.
http://www.euractive.com/Article?tcmuri=tcm:29-137076-16&type=News

Feldman, A. **"Surviving Sox."** *Inc. Magazine*, September 2005.
http://www.inc.com/magazine/20050901/surviving-so.html

Fennell, T. **"The next 50 years."** *CA Magazine*, April 2005.
http://www.camagazine.com/index.cfm/ci_id/25675/la_id/1.html

**"Five emerging trends will resurge global banking in next decade."** IBM, 15 November 2005.
http://biz.yahoo.com/iw/051115/0101035.html

Garten, J.E. **"A new threat to America Inc."** *Business Week*, 25 July 2005.
http://www.businessweek.com/magazine/content/05_30/b3944123.htm

**"The Global Economic and Financial Impact of an Avian Flu Pandemic and the Role of the IMF."** Avian Flu Working Group, International Monetary Fund. 28 February 2006.

**"Glocalisation: a new route to world peace."** Deutsche Presse-Agentur, 19 May 2003.
http://www.wordspy.com/words/glocalisation.asp

**"Glocalisation."** Wikipedia.
http://en.wikipedia.org/wiki/Glocalisation

**"Google: Brazil among the most interesting emerging markets."** TCM Net, 31 January 2006.
http://www.tmcnet.com/usubmit/2006/01/31/1329456.htm

Gordon, J. **"The Kondratieff Wave: June 1789 through October 2003."** The Long Wave Analyst, 2003.
http://www.thelongwaveanalyst.ca

Howarth, F. **"Basel II compliance: another burden for European CSOs?"** Bloor Research, 16 August 2005.
http://www.it-analysis.com/business/compliance/content.php?cid=8031

Howell, D. **"Hey, young spender."** *The Guardian*, 30 June 2005.
http://technology.guardian.co.uk/online/businesssolutions/story/0,12581,1517197,00.html

Hunter, M. **"Senate approves rise in debt ceiling."** CNS News, 16 March 2006.
http://www.cnsnews.com/ViewPolitics.asp?Page=%5CPolitics%5Carchive%5C200603%5CPOL20060316b.html

**"ICT's role crucial for the achievement of the Lisbon Strategy."** Euractive, 1 February, 2006.
http://europa.eu.int/rapid/pressReleasesAction.do?reference=IP/06/108&forat=HTML&aged=0&language=EN&guilanguage=en

**"IMF says bird flu pandemic would have serious impact on global economy."** *Forbes*, 11 April 2006.
http://www.forbes.com/finance/feeds/afx/2006/04/11/afx2662979.html

Jaques, R. **"Global banks' ICT not ready for Basel."** *CT Week*, 29 June 2004.
http://www.ctweek.co.uk/vnunet/news/2125360/global-banks-ready-basel- ii?vnu_lt=itw_art_related_articles

Jardin, X. **"Web 2.0 cracks start to show."** *Wired*, 27 October 2005.
http://www.wired.com/news/technology/0,1282,69366.html

Jubaks, J. **"Has Congress sparked a banking crunch?"** MSN Money, 6 September 2005.
http://moneycentral.sn.com/content/MP127636.asp

Kanellos, M. **"Move over, China: a new powerhouse is emerging."** CNET News, 27 June 2005.
http://news.com.com/India+renaissance+Move+over,+China/2009-1041_3-5751994.html

Kaste, M. **"Brazil's agriculture boom exacts high cost."** NPR, January 2005.
http://www.npr.org/templates/story/story.php?storyId=4465096

**"Katrina may cost as much as four years of war."** MSNBC News, 10 September 2005.
http://www.msnbc.msn.com/id/9281409

Kerevan, G. **"Europe's baby boomers will lose edge to the US millennium generation."** 8 February 2006.
http://uk.biz.yahoo.com/08022006/17/europe-s-baby-boomers-lose-edge-millennium-generation.html

Kirkup, J. **"Bird flu: the secret Cabinet document."** *The Scotsman*, 3 April 2006.
http://news.scotsman.com/health.cfm?id=508792006

Lemagnen, M. **"Emerging markets plan tech take-off."** *FDI Magazine*, 20 October 2004.
http://www.fdimagazine.com/news/fullstory.php/aid/833/Emerging_markets_plan_tech_take-off.html

Lyman, P. & Varian, H.R. **"Berkeley Study: How much information?"** 2003.
http://www.sims.berkeley.edu:8000/research/projects/how-much-info-2003

MacManns, R. **"Mashups: who's really in control?"** ZDNet, 2 March 2006.
http://blogs.zdnet.com/web2explorer/?p=128

Maiden, M. **"The tidal wave of retiring baby boomers."** 19 December 2005.
http://www.theage.com/au/news/malcolm-maiden/the-tidal-wave-of-retiring-baby-bomers/2005/1218/1134840739313.html

**"Mapping the Global Future."** National Intelligence Council, December 2004.

**"Mash-up."** Wikipedia.
http://en.wikipedia.org/wiki/Mashup(web_application_hybrid)

Mills, E. **"Mapping a revolution with 'mashups.'"** CNET News, 17 November 2005.
http://news.com.com/Mapping+a+revolution+with+mashups/2009-1025_3-5944608.html

**"Money supply."** Wikipedia.
http://en.wikipedia.org/wiki/Money_Supply

Mortleman, J. **"Skills shortage creates Basel II compliance fears."** VNU Net, 9 August 2004.
http://www.vnunet.com/vnunet/news/2125638/skills-shortage-creates-basel-ii-compliance-fears?vnu_lt=vnu_art_related_articles

Nacamuli, A. **"How European banks can prepare for SEPA."** GT News, 25 July.
http://www.gtnews.com/article/6051.cfm

**"The new retirement survey from Merrill Lynch reveals how baby boomers will transform retirement."**
Merrill Lynch, 22 February 2005.
http://www.ml.com/index.asp?id=7695_7696_8149_46028_46503_46635

O'Reilly, T. **"What is Web 2.0—design patterns & business models for the next generation of software."**
O'Reilly Net, 30 September 2005.
http://www.oreillynet.com/pub/a/oreilly/tim/news/2005/09/30/what-is-web-20.html

**"Peak oil."** Wikipedia.
http://en.wikipedia.org/wiki/Peak_oil.

Prahalad, C.K. **The Fortune at the Bottom of the Pyramid.** Wharton School Publishing: Philadelphia. 2005.

**"Q&A: EU's Lisbon Agenda."** BBC News, 22 March 2005.
http://news.bbc.co.uk/2/hi/business/4373485.stm

Ratnesar, R. **"Generation Europe."** *Time Europe*, 2003.
http://www.time.com/time/europe/generatione/stories

Rebelo, P. **"Brazil's bumpy road to the low-cost PC."** CNET News, 3 November 2005.
http:news.com.com/Brazils+bumpy+road+to+the+low-cost+PC/2100-1041_3-5928985.html

Reid, T. **"US spends its way to 28 Eiffel Towers: made out of pure gold."** Times Online, March 2006.
http://www.timesonline.co.uk/article/0,11069-2090441,00.html

Richburg, K. **"A generation on the move in Europe."** Global Policy, 22 July 2003.
http://www.globalpolicy.org/nations/sovereign/integrate/2003/0723youth.htm

Rip, P. **"Some problems with mashups."** Early Stage VC, February 2006.
http://earlystagevc.typepad.com/earlystagevc/2006/02/the_problems_wi.html

**"Rising powers: the changing geopolitical landscape."** CIA National Intelligence Council 2020 Project, December 2004.

**"Sarbanes-Oxley in the EU."** Managing Credit, Receivables & Collections, All Business. June 2005.
http://www.allbusiness.com/periodicals/article/458628-1.html

**"Salesforce.com. receives Intelligent Enterprise 2008 Editors' Choice award."** Successforce Community.
http://blog.crmsuccess.com/crmsuccess/mashups/index.html

Savinar, M. **"Life after the oil crash."**
http://www.lifeaftertheoilcrash.net

Spiegler, M. **"Glocalisation: easier said than done."** *The Industry Standard*, 9 October 2000.
http://www.thestandard.com/article/0,1902,18890,00.html

Surowiecki, J. **"In yuan we trust."** *The New Yorker*, 18 April 2005.
http://www.newyorker.com/talk/content/articles/050418ta_talk_Surowiecki

**"Ten things you need to know about pandemic influenza."** World Health Organisation, 14 October 2005.
http://www.who.int/csr/disease/influenza/pandemic10things/en

Terdiman, D. **"Wells Fargo launches game inside 'Second Life.'"** ZDNet 15 September 2006.
http://news.zdnet.com/2100-1040_21-5868030.html

Turley, J.S. **"Get ready for EU's 8th Directive."** Ernst & Young, June 2004.

Vail, J. **"A peak behind the curtain."** Rhizome, 10 December 2005.
http://www.jeffvail.net/2005/12/peak-behind-curtain.html

Watson, J. **"UK banks face rising bill for Basel II."** *ICT Week*, 27 July 2005.
http://www.itweek.co.uk/computing/news/2140432/uk-banks-face-rising-bill-basel

Watson, J. **"Costs likely to rise for single payments area plan."** VNU Net, 1 June 2005.
http://www.vnunet.com/computing/news/2137402/costs-likely-rise-single-payments-area-plan

# About the author

For the last 12 years Daniel Erasmus has been facilitating scenario processes for diverse clients across three continents. As founder and director of the DTN, Daniel leads a consulting firm that specialises in scenario thinking and transformation processes, and licenses early warning systems to organisations interested in looking ahead. With an international team of staff members and associates, Daniel has worked with a range of private and public sector clients that include Nokia, Rabobank, the City of Rotterdam, the Rijksgebouwendienst, Schlumberger, Telenor and Vodafone.

Daniel pioneered the use of scenarios to facilitate deep dialogue about the changing information society and its impact on our organisations, work and societies. The initial ideas were sowed in "A common language for strategy," an article he authored for the 1999 *Financial Times* series, Mastering Information Technology. Since 1996 he has facilitated more than 100 scenario sets on these issues, ranging from the future of organisations in an information society to the future of the global village.

The strategic initiatives, resulting from the DTN scenarios, have facilitated € 400 million in additional valuation for its clients since 2001. Among others, the DTN scenarios anticipated the rise of the Internet, the long recession following the dot.com crash, the delay in 3G implementation and the dominance of WiFi, the failure of WAP and the success of SMS, a $70 oil price at a time when it was $23, the foundering of the European constitution, and shifts in television viewing patterns.

In addition to his consulting work, Daniel is a Visiting Professor at the Ashridge Business School and a Fellow at The Rotterdam School of Management. As a lecturer, he has taught scenario thinking to more than 1000 executives and post-graduate MBA students at companies and business schools, ranging in location from Helsinki to Cape Town, and from Paris to Seoul.

Born in Cape Town, South Africa, Daniel lives in Amsterdam with his wife Elisabeth and three daughters, who are, he is convinced, the most beautiful in the world! He can be found as often in his office in Amsterdam as on planes, trains and in cafes with his laptop, a ristretto and a yearning for the warm plains of Africa.

dtn.net
scenariothinking.org
danielerasmus.org